A Lifetime of Hunting and Fishing

The Ones That Got Away and the Ones That Didn't

George A. Smith

A Lifetime of Hunting and Fishing

ISBN 978-1-943424-24-5

Library of Congress Control Number: 2017949046

Permission has been granted by *The Maine Sportsman* magazine for use of stories written by the author and published in their magazine.

North Country Press
Unity, Maine

This book must be dedicated to my dad, Ezra Smith, who inspired me to be a Maine sportsman and spent six decades hunting and fishing with me. Many of my stories are his stories too. I also want to dedicate this book to my children, Rebekah, Joshua, and Hilary; my grandchildren, Addison, Vishal, Ada, and Esme, all of whom spend time outdoors with me; and to my wife, Linda, who was a hunter's widow during many hunting and fishing seasons, but who also took up fly fishing to join me on the lake at camp and who even enjoyed fly fishing adventures with me in Alaska and Quebec.

Introduction

This is a collection of stories written over the last 30 years about my lifetime of hunting and fishing in Maine, plus my hunting and fishing adventures in Labrador, Quebec, Montana, North Dakota, and Alaska, along with other outdoor adventures and even a few fictional stories.

I've been blessed many times over by the opportunities to enjoy my favorite pursuits, both in my free time and for work. Yes, hunting and fishing were part of my work life. Lucky me!

These stories were written at various times over the past 30 years, and I have not attempted to update them. I hope that is not too confusing. They are presented, just as they were written, back in the day.

Table of Contents

Walk my wood lot with me

Hunting with a friend on my woodlot in November, I found myself stopping often to tell him a story about something that happened at that spot. Thinking about it later, I decided that would be a good way to share my hunting stories with you. So let's begin to do that today, starting right in my home office.

My 150-acre woodlot is located between Hopkins Stream and Route 41, while my house is a quarter-mile away on Blake Hill Road. The woodlot is dedicated to my dad. Up on Route 41 is a sign: The Ezra Smith Wildlife Conservation Area. I access my lot from Route 41, by canoeing down the stream, or by crossing the road from my house and hunting through the woodlots of two of my neighbors until I get to my woodlot.

On the phone

I've got a few good stories, en route to my woodlot. One afternoon I was sitting at my desk, talking on the phone to Chris Potholm, when I spotted a huge buck crossing the side lawn between the house and the stream. I slammed down the phone without even saying goodbye to Chris, threw on my hunting jacket, grabbed my rifle, and dashed out the door to follow the buck that had crossed the road and entered my neighbor's woodlot.

Following the buck's track, I went up a ridge to a small group of firs situated right next to one of my tree stands. And I did a double take, spotting the rear end of a deer sticking out of the firs. Quickly realizing the deer was too small to be my big buck, I laughed. Apparently, the deer thought it was hidden. Hearing my laugh, the deer took one leap deeper into the firs and disappeared, while I returned to the house and called Chris back to apologize for hanging up on him. Given that he's an avid hunter too, he understood perfectly my frantic haste to get out after that buck, which I never saw again.

In the tree stand

While we're at this spot on my neighbor's woodlot, let me tell you about what happened one day while I was sitting in that same tree stand and had another disappointing encounter with a big buck. The stand overlooks a small knoll, on the other side of which is a woods trail. I could see a small piece of the trail before it went behind the knoll, and then a longer section of the trail after it emerged from behind the knoll closer to my stand.

One afternoon, a big buck came sauntering along on the trail. I figured I'd have my best shot when he emerged on the other side of the knoll, so I watched him disappear behind the knoll and got my gun up ready to shoot when he came back into view.

And I waited, and waited, and waited. But while he was behind the knoll, he'd turned off the trail and headed north toward the bog. More than 30 years later, I can still see that buck. You never forget the ones that got away!

I was in that stand another time when four does walked into the clearing. It was one of those years when we couldn't shoot does, so all I could do was admire those deer. But I did that with a smile on my face.

Trembling hunter

Let's continue on toward my woodlot. Right here, where you see the rock wall that separates the woodlots of my two neighbors, I used to like to sit on the wall right up there on the rise. A deer trail emerges into a small open area just 40 yards beyond my seat, and one early morning I heard a deer approaching on that trail. When the deer began to walk into the opening where I'd have a shot, I nearly choked. He was huge! What a rack!

At that point in my hunting life, I'd never shot a big buck, and I began trembling. Really badly. The buck was moving very slowly, and I got off four quick shots, never troubling him at all. In fact, he stopped and looked my way after my fourth shot. I took a very big breath and calmed down enough to get off a final shot.

As he took off, I did too, searching for any sign that I'd hit him. Nothing. Nada. No hair. No blood. Five shots and I'd missed him on all five. I was distraught and followed in the direction he'd run for a hundred yards, still seeing no sign that he'd been hit, then returned to the house where I was scheduled to meet Dad for a morning hunt.

I told Dad my sad, sad story, and despite the fact he thought we should go back and make sure I'd missed, I was certain I had, so we hunted elsewhere until lunch. But after lunch, Dad insisted we go back there to hunt for the buck. And about 200 yards down the trail he'd taken, we discovered a spot where he'd lain down and bled. I'd hit him, all right. We were able to follow his tracks to where he swam across the stream, and I spent the rest of that day and two days after that on the other side of the stream, hunting for him, without luck.

That's the only deer I ever wounded and lost, and the regret remains strong. But I learned a valuable lesson, never again giving up on a deer I'd shot at.

Too much rain

OK, we're moving into my other neighbor's woodlot now, and just a couple hundred yards from that stone wall – that spot you can see right there by that cluster of big rocks – toward the end of the hunting day one year, my dad shot a big doe. A really big doe.

At that point in our hunting careers, we went out in any weather and it was raining hard that afternoon. While Dad had hit the deer hard, the blood trail ran out quickly, probably washed away in the rain, and darkness set in quickly, so we retreated to the house, determined to come back the next morning and look for the deer. We did that, with no luck.

Two days later, hunting with Dad and my friend, Harry Vanderweide, I stumbled onto the dead doe in the bog. Dad insisted on cleaning it, dragging it out of the woods, and taking it to the Mount Vernon Country Store to tag it. I thought that was noble, for sure, because from the smell, we knew the deer was spoiled.

Dead coyote

We're sitting behind a small ledge now, and just over there to the left you can see a large grouping of boulders. Porcupines reside in the crevices under the boulders, and one year I found a dead coyote there. The coyote hadn't been dead long and I have no idea what killed it. You see so many amazing things while you're hunting.

Straight ahead you can see a bench, next to a vernal pool. All kinds of critters come to that pool, so this is a great place to sit. My woodlot starts right at the vernal pool. And if you look to the right, deer exit the bog there. I used to sit over there, closer to the bog, and I did shoot a doe there one year.

Between that group of boulders on the left and the stream, hunting back toward my house one day, I jumped a deer. Luckily, there was enough snow so I could follow it, and it headed upstream, getting almost to where you could see my house. Then it turned left and headed toward Route 41. I assumed it would cross the road and be gone. But amazingly, just before it got to Route 41, it turned left again and headed south, running now between the bog and the road.

"This is great," I thought. Dad was sitting about a quarter mile away on a ridge overlooking the bog. And the deer was headed right for him. I took just a few steps in the new direction when I heard Dad fire two shots. Turns out the buck had burst out of the bushes and gotten all the way past him before he was able to get his gun up and fire. The buck dropped right there. The six-pointer weighed 155 pounds. And this is where it gets really interesting.

Two days later, I was sitting high up in a hemlock tree when a small buck came up from the stream and walked right up to me. I took a shot and missed, but the buck, not knowing where the shot came from, backed up and stood behind another hemlock. Then he stepped out again and I dropped him right there. He weighed 155 pounds and had a 6-point rack – identical to Dad's buck! No bragging rights that year!

Running into the woods after a funeral

Nothing is more important to deer hunting than spending lots of time in an area you hunt. I'm on my woodlot year-round and spend a huge amount of time there hunting deer in November and December. I know my deer, where and when to find them, and how to hunt them. This story happened right on this knoll, and is one I have used in the past to illustrate this point: Even if you only have a very brief amount of time on any given day, get out there in the woods with your gun.

The November 15th funeral of a distant relative had been at 2 p.m. And as family and friends gathered for refreshments and fellowship afterward, my thoughts drifted to the woods. I'd been stalking a particular buck most of the season, catching only a single glimpse of him the first week. The print he'd left two days before near my tree stand in the bog measured 4 ½ inches in length and I knew he had a gorgeous rack.

As I excused myself from the gathering at 3 p.m., a decision was reached. After sitting for hours in two different tree stands without a glimpse of my buck, I knew I needed to get farther into the woods. On a tiny knoll, cut over about five years before but still holding a few oak trees and a good nut crop, the buck had left three fresh scrapes earlier that week. I wanted to be on that knoll that afternoon.

Time was short. Arriving home at 3:30 p.m., changing quickly from dark suit to fluorescent orange, I grabbed my .30-06 and literally ran the half-mile to the knoll, arriving at 3:45 p.m. in a sweat, trying to catch my breath. I took a position on the edge of the knoll, hiding myself downwind within those small firs over there by that big boulder.

At 3:55 p.m., two cracks behind me in the thick pines put me on alert. I let off the safety on my rifle and watched. Five minutes later, I saw him. Head down, passing between the pines about 150 feet to my right. His rack was huge! And just like that, he was gone. Instead of coming toward me, he went down the knoll to the stream. But before serious depression could set in, he was back, moving my way through some thick firs.

Buck fever set in. Sweat reappeared on my brow. The beginning of serious shaking was apparent in the limbs. Flashbacks to a similar opportunity missed the previous season danced through my head. A stand of six or eight small firs stood between the buck and me. He sauntered along for what seemed an eternity, head to the ground, eating acorns.

Every few feet, he'd lift his head and those antlers would appear above the firs, a vision I have often seen in my dreams. The old limbs began to shake more vigorously. I could only see him when the antlers rose above the firs, so there was nothing to shoot at.

Finally, he stepped out from behind that huge boulder, just 30 yards away. I'd already taken aim at that spot, eye glued to the scope. When he filled the scope, I fired. BANG! He was off, cutting across the knoll right there in front of me. I fired two wild and useless shots before he fell, about 75 feet from where my first shot had broken his forward left shoulder and ripped up both lungs.

You've seen those TV commercials where the customer leaps into the air: "Wow, what a feeling!" That was me. Deep in the woods. Dancing around my buck. He was a beaut. It was really the first time I ever picked out a particular deer, stuck with him, trying to figure out his every habit and movement, finally outwitting him. It's an extraordinary feeling.

I found his stomach full of cedar and partridge berry leaves. He was lean, dressing out at 175 pounds, but his 8-point rack was magnificent. He turned out to be very tasty and tender. The head hangs in my office today, thanks to the good work of Dave Cote who had a taxidermy business in Winslow.

Before I finished cleaning the buck, darkness had set in. I hauled him 200 yards to the stream, which you can see down there below us, picked up my canoe stashed nearby, loaded him in, and paddled home. Linda and my 2 ½-year-old son Josh were at the bridge, looking for me. When Linda shined her flashlight into the canoe, Josh shouted, "Nice deer, Dad! Good fishing!"

Good fishing indeed!

Up next

OK, now let's move down toward the stream. On that knoll over there, I shot my Thanksgiving Day buck. I've told you that story before, probably several times! And you see my tree stand over there in that stand of oaks? Well, wait 'til you hear the stories of the deer I've seen from that stand!

OK, we're approaching my tree stand among these nice oaks, but let me tell you one story that happened before Harry Vanderweide and I put the tree stand up here. I was following this same path we are on, and arrived at the high point, right here, where you can see the stream down below. Noting movement on my left down by the stream, I saw a big buck with the most unusual set of antlers I've ever seen. It looked like something you'd see on cattle, very wide with just two points.

The buck was walking up the hill toward me, and as he got within about 100 yards, I got my rifle up and ready to shoot, following him in my scope. When he turned broadside to me, heading back down toward the stream, I fired, and he took off. Certain I'd hit him, I raced down to the spot where he'd been when

I shot, and all I found was a tiny bit of hair. I'd shot right through a very thick tree! It looked like the bullet had exited the tree but barely troubled the buck. I followed his tracks to where he swam across the stream and saw nothing that indicated I'd hurt him.

So, why don't you climb up into the tree stand and take a look around. What do you think? Yes, you have a great view from up there! There's a well-worn deer trail to your left, down toward the stream, and another to your right, between this ridge and the next. I'm not exaggerating when I say I see two dozen or more deer here every hunting season. Sometimes they hang out for quite a while, eating the acorns or chewing on cedar trees. I could spend a couple hours here telling you stories about this spot, but I'll limit this to two of my favorites.

Cutting off my finger

I still think of it as the buck's revenge. I shot a 160-pound buck from the stand, just before dark, and it ran a hundred yards past me before dropping dead. By the time I got around to cleaning it out, it was pretty dark, so I was hurrying. Big mistake.

My left hand was inside the deer when my right hand moved inside with the knife. Although I didn't feel any pain, I knew immediately that I'd taken a nice slice out of my finger. Pulling my hands out of the deer, blood spurted all over the place. And I could not stop the flow.

So I abandoned the deer, wrapped my finger in a handkerchief, and hurried down to the canoe, paddling swiftly downstream, blood dripping down the oar and into the canoe. At the landing I jumped into my vehicle and drove home. But even there, I could not stop the bleeding, so I left Linda a note: "Don't worry about the blood on the floor. I'm OK. Headed to the hospital to stitch up a knife wound."

The emergency room doc did a nice job with the stitching, gave me some antibiotics, and wrapped my entire left hand in a big bandage. The next day my neighbor, Ron LaRue, and my dad went back into the woods with me to retrieve the deer. I'd worried a bit that coyotes would get at it, but they hadn't. And the photo of the deer in the back of Dad's truck, with my hand in a huge bandage, is one of my favorites.

Saw him three times

My favorite story from this spot happened the year I saw the same buck three times. The first time, I heard something about 200 yards behind the tree stand, and when I turned to see what it was, the buck saw me and took off.

The second time I saw him is an amazing story. I was sitting in the stand reading a book when I heard a commotion. I looked up to see a doe sprinting through the woods right toward me, with that same buck following close behind. I grabbed my gun, but they were running fast and were already right in front of me when they turned and passed right below my stand. I aimed the gun down toward the buck and fired, a clean miss. And before I could even take a breath, they were gone. Yes, I was kind of disappointed when I trudged home that night.

But a week later, I looked up from my book to see that same buck walking leisurely my way, coming up from the stream. When he got right beside me, no more than 50 yards away, I shot him. Three times was the charm!

Well, get down out of the stand, and let's move up toward my stand of big hemlocks. Got some great stories from up there, too.

—

This stand of hemlocks up there in front of us is one of my very favorite spots. Lots of interesting stories occurred here. Over here on the right, I now have a folding chair. The deer exit the bog right here and walk down toward the stream. I used to have a ground blind down there below us.

One afternoon I was sitting in that blind reading a book, when I heard a doe bleat. I couldn't see either the doe or fawn, but I figured out that they were headed my way. And I never did see the fawn, but the doe walked right by my blind, close enough so I could have touched her. When she got right beside me, I spoke to her, and boy, did she come right off the ground!

One of my favorite stories here happened when I was sitting high up in that hemlock tree over there. You can see my ladder up against the tree over there. Until the limbs started to rot, I climbed the tree from limb to limb. Eventually the lower limbs rotted, so I put up the ladder. Come over here, I want to show you where I sat. Yup, way up there. You can see a great place where I could sit on one limb, place my feet on a lower limb, and have a third limb right there to steady my rifle.

Well, I was up there one early morning when I spotted a small buck coming my way from the stream. He was quite a distance, but turned when he got to the other side of this hemlock stand and made his way toward me. I actually stood up in the tree to take the shot, and missed.

He didn't know where the shot came from, so he backed up and stood behind that big hemlock over there. I could just see his head sticking out. So I aimed there, and darned if he didn't step forward right into the open. That time I didn't miss. Dad was up on the other side of the bog and heard me shoot. Another great hunting day for us.

Last year I posted my woodlot, primarily because it was getting quite a few hunters I didn't know. And I wanted my neighbors, the Brickett family, to hunt here, along with my guests. Early in the season, Mrs. Brickett got a small buck back where we were sitting behind that ledge. And then, the next to last Friday, I heard a knock on the door about 6:00 p.m., and there stood 17-year-old Justin Brickett, with a huge smile on his face.

He'd been sitting in these hemlocks when the huge buck we'd been seeing in my yard came along. He downed it with a single shot. It was a nice 8-point, 185-pound buck, and honestly, I've never seen a hunter so excited. As Justin showed me his photos, I shared that excitement. Really, I couldn't have imagined a better outcome for a hunt on my woodlot.

I'll tell you one more story before we move on. The deer sometimes like to bed down on hummocks in the grass along the stream. You can see the stream from here. Well, right out there, just about opposite where we're standing, I was canoeing my brother-in-law Dom Spadea downstream when I saw a huge buck jump up out of the swale grass and take off toward the woods.

I quickly turned the canoe toward shore and urged Dom to shoot. Watching the buck, I could have shot him easily, but Dom was between me and the deer, and I really wanted him to get it anyway. But he didn't shoot. When the buck got to the alders, he turned and stared at us. I almost jumped into the stream to take a shot at him. Turns out that Dom, sitting in the front of the canoe, couldn't see the buck over the tall swale grass in front of him.

I've got another Dom story coming up, when we get out of these hemlocks and cross over a small brook that drains my bog.

———

You can hop across the brook on those two big rocks. Now, up ahead here, you can see the remains of the first tree stand I built on this woodlot. Dom once had four deer run by him right there, and he shot the fourth one. It looked like a good spot on the edge of this cutting on our left and the bog on our right, so I immediately put up that stand. It was nice and big, and I had a very comfortable seat. The only problem was that I never saw a deer from that stand. Never.

I did see moose, often. Once, three young bull moose wandered past me, and another time a huge bull moose came along. He sensed that something was in the stand, so he sauntered over to see what it was. His antlers were close enough to touch, just below my feet and the stand's floor. When he looked up at me,

I said, "Hello, Mr. Moose!" But that didn't alarm him. He just turned slowly and ambled off into the bog.

Now we need to get through this thicket, and then we'll emerge in one of my favorite places. OK, here we are, a nice stand of hardwoods. This stand pokes out into the bog. You can see the bog over there on our left, and also over here on our right. There's a deer bedding area in the bog on the left, and when we jump them out of there, instead of staying in the bog and running around this stand, they run into the stand to cross it and re-enter the bog on the other side, over here behind us.

Dad and I have both shot deer here. We would take turns walking through the bog and jumping the deer out of their beds, while the other sat over here in that chair. It was a very effective way to hunt.

My best story here is the time I took a DIF&W fisheries biologist who lived in Mount Vernon, out hunting. We canoed upstream and cut through the woods to this spot, and I placed him right there behind those trees in that seat.

I swung up through the cutting to the south of us, then plunged into the bog and carefully hunted my way through it until I approached the bedding area. Sure enough, I caught a glimpse of a nice buck when he took one jump and ran away right toward my friend. I waited for the shot, and waited, and waited. Finally, I walked out, astonished that he hadn't gotten a shot at that buck.

He was very excited. He'd seen the buck emerge from the bog into the hardwoods, headed right for him. "Why didn't you shoot?" I asked. "Well, I was waiting for it to run by me, but it turned and ran back into the bog," he said. The buck had been no more than 75 yards away. Yes, I was flabbergasted.

I headed north, staying in the woods that parallel the bog, then plunged into the bog again and hunted back toward my friend. And sure enough, I jumped that buck again and drove him out into the hardwoods. This time my friend was ready and he fired as soon as he saw the buck, dropping it in its tracks. It was an 8-pointer, and if I remember correctly, it weighed about 180 pounds.

Well, let's hike through the bog. I want to show you how to get across it, and I've got more stories for when we get to the other side where my woodlot meets Route 41. Careful of your steps now. There's quite a bit of water in the bog this time of year.

Careful – a really big pothole of water is coming up. Isn't this bog nice? My property line is just off to the right of us. At this spot, in the middle of the bog, I once had a ladder stand. Never saw a deer there, but did have a moose walk by me. Over there to the left is where a cow moose once tried to run me over. Apparently, I'd gotten between her and her calf. As you can see, there are no tall trees here, so all I could do was jump sideways into the brush. She charged by me, kicking up her hind legs, no more than 6 feet away. Not sure if I could have gotten away with shooting her in self-defense! But it was a close call.

OK, so we're out of the bog, and you can see the steep hill ahead that takes us to the road. Let's walk along the edge of the bog here. I want to show you my tree stand, just below the cemetery. I've chased a lot of deer through here. You can see this deer trail that comes down the hill. The deer cross the road up there and come down the hill this way. Dad used to like to sit up there, just off the trail, behind a big rock. One opening day, he shot a nice doe there, but couldn't find it. We met at the house for breakfast, and Dad, my then 8-year-old son Josh, and I went back to look for the deer. Josh found the deer in a hole over there toward the tree stand.

So, there's the stand, and I've got a great story about it. My friend Harry Vanderweide's adult daughter, Amanda, decided she wanted to start hunting. For her first hunting season I put that stand up for her. I told her to watch the bog down below her, because that's where the deer would emerge, and that they'd walk right up to her, then turn left and walk this trail that you and I are on.

Well, sure enough, on opening day, the big buck we'd been seeing around the house and woodlot walked out of the bog, right where I'd said he would. He walked up and under Amanda's stand, turned left and headed up the trail, stopping and turning broadside about 50 yards up the trail. Amanda was shaking so badly that she never even got off a shot! She redeemed herself a couple of years later by making a terrific shot on a nice spikehorn, hunting with Harry and me in Fayette.

One time I was walking up the road to get to this stand when a bunch of deer trotted out into the road right in front of me. It was pitch black, but they saw me and split up. Half turned around and went back up the hill, and the other half ran into my woodlot. I sat down there, hoping the other deer would come back that way, but they didn't.

Dad

OK, I've got one last story for you, and I want to end these stories where I started. My woodlot is named for Dad, who hunted with me for 53 years. Dad was pretty feeble in November 2013, but he was determined to hunt. And he somehow got all the way from the road down to the bottom of this hill on the edge of the bog, where he wanted to sit. And that's where I found him, astonished that he thought he could get back up the hill. Well, it took more than an hour to do that, even though it was only about 300 yards up to the road. Several times he had to stop and rest, and for the final 25 yards, he crawled. It brought tears to my eyes.

After that, we put a chair over there, just a little way into the woods from the road, and another chair at Steep Hill Farm in Fayette where we loved to hunt. Dad enjoyed sitting in both chairs. He died the night before the firearms season on deer opened in 2014, and I've often said he died that night because he was so upset he couldn't get out hunting the next day.

We've left both chairs in place in Dad's memory. Come this way, I want to show you Dad's chair here on my woodlot. OK, there it is. You can see there's a nice deer trail passing right by the chair, and from here you have a nice view down the hill toward the bog. That 2014 season, my first without Dad, I pasted his photo on this chair and instructed him to send a big buck down to the tree stand for me. The second Saturday of that season, I was passing by Dad's chair when I noticed a very fresh, very large ground scrape, left by a big deer, right beside the chair. "Dad," I said, "you were supposed to send that buck my way!"

These days, I wear a piece of Dad's clothing anytime I'm hunting, so he's still with me. And I will never forget all the wonderful hunts we had here, on my woodlot, and elsewhere. Come with me down to the Olde Post Office Café, we'll grab some lunch and I'll tell you some more stories. Got some really good ones about a couple of hunts on the North Wayne farm where Dad grew up.

Best bucks (and does) and hunts

With thanks to Dad

I was born a Maine sportsman, raised a Maine sportsman, and will die a Maine sportsman. Thanks to Dad. Just like Dad. My first memories are of pheasants, rabbits, setters, and beagles. Or course, before that, there was the hunter safety course and lots of shooting at the range of my dad's club. Ezra Smith insisted on that.

We raised English setters and used them to hunt the pheasants that Dad's club raised and put out all over Readfield, Winthrop, and Monmouth. I've never forgotten the experience of shooting my first pheasant, with Dad right beside me in a field at the end of Maranacook Lake. In that exact spot, there's now a house.

We also had beagles and I absolutely loved rabbit hunting, the cold mornings, the trudge through the snow into the woods, usually on Memorial Drive. The baying of the beagle and the knowledge that the pursued rabbit would run in a circle and pass right by me if I got into the right spot was electrifying. Occasionally, I even shot one.

Dad also taught me to trap. Early mornings before school, he always accompanied me to check my traps on a nearby stream. It was so exciting to find a muskrat in a trap. And we returned to that same stream to hunt ducks. I have a vision of a flock of black ducks flying low over our decoys and Dad saying, "Shoot!" We shot at the same time and each got a duck.

But deer hunting put us in the woods together the most. And, ironically, it was the sport in which I was least successful. At least initially. I didn't shoot my first deer until I was 25 years old. I'm remembering that there weren't that many deer in the 1960s – but that may be fanciful thinking.

Dad introduced me to deer hunting on his old farm in North Wayne and in 2013, we hunted there for the 53rd year. That's where I shot the Thanksgiving buck. It's my favorite deer hunting story. I was sitting on a bucket in the woods behind an old cemetery and Dad was hunting his way up over a ridge from the farm, toward me.

It was a very cold and icy day, and I heard the tromp, tromp, tromp of a deer coming from a long way off. I got the gun up, aimed for a small opening in the trees, and when the deer – a huge buck – stepped into the opening, I shot.

Tromp, tromp, tromp, he continued on his way. I had missed. As the family gathered mid-day for a Thanksgiving feast, I was morose. Worst Thanksgiving ever.

The next day we decided to try it again. I had moved slightly to have a better shot if a deer came up over the ridge. Thirty minutes after I sat down on the bucket, I heard him coming. Tromp, tromp, tromp. I was sure it was the same big buck. And it was. And this time, I hit him.

But he continued for a ways, so I shot him again, and he ran straight into a tree and flipped completely upside down. Dad said he could hear me hollering, even though he was several hundred yards down over the ridge. Best day-after-Thanksgiving ever. Particularly because Dad was there with me.

Eventually, I purchased a woodlot in Mount Vernon and we started hunting there. One year we shot nice bucks two days apart.

I got the first one, a 155-pounder. Two days later, Dad was sitting in one of our favorite spots when a buck burst out of the bushes and ran right at Dad. His buck weighed 155 pounds, too.

Eventually, as Dad and I got older, the hunters' breakfasts became as much a part of our tradition as the hunt. But every year, one or both of us would get a deer, and we piled up story after story after story. Some were pretty amazing, like the time Dad was sitting just outside the bog, watching a ground scrape, when a spike horn walked up to him and he shot it. Before he could even get out of his seat, a huge buck came along, following the spike horn.

I returned to that seat the next day, and sure enough, the big buck came back. I was reading a novel when I looked up and he was straddling the scrape. I put the book down, picked up the rifle and shot him. He weighed 196 pounds and had a beautiful rack.

And then there was our last year. Dad was hurting but determined to hunt. I put a chair up near the road, at the top of the steep hill that leads down into my bog, and told him to sit there while I thrashed around in the bog. But he trudged all the way down the hill. When I found him there, it took over an hour, with a lot of stops, to get him up the 200 yards to the road. I knew then it would be our last year of hunting together.

Dad was in the Hospice Unit at the Togus VA hospital, unable to hunt that next fall. But he hadn't given up fishing. Maine's Department of Inland Fisheries and Wildlife stocks a small pond on the hospital campus for the patients. I took Dad there five times and casting from his wheelchair, he caught brook trout. For sure, at the age of 91 and in poor health, he was still a Maine sportsman – and we were able to create more wonderful memories.

The opening day of deer season the month after he died wasn't the same. But I returned to our favorite spots, thought a lot about Dad, and let the memories flow.

A doe, a deer, a female deer

On the first day of firearms season on deer, I responded to a request from a neighbor to do something about a wounded deer that swam across Hopkins Pond and dropped on the shore. My neighbor had watched it from her kitchen window and was concerned and upset.

I picked up her husband and we drove around to the site and located the deer, a spike horn. When it jumped up, the deer was in obvious distress, so I shot it, registered it, and gave it to my neighbors to butcher and eat.

This was not how I'd envisioned my deer hunting season opener, but it was the right thing to do. For the rest of the season, I was unable to shoot a buck. But a bonus doe permit allowed me to continue hunting, although I had hoped to save that permit for the muzzle-loading season that follows the regular firearms season.

If this sounds like a long hunting season, my wife Linda would agree as would Cate Pineau, wife of my hunting buddy Ed. By way of confession, Ed and I hunted more than half the days of the deer season. We haven't yet informed our wives that coyotes can be hunted all winter.

One of the ironies of the decrease in the number of hunting participants is that those of us who do hunt have more opportunities than ever before. Imagine, this year I harvested two turkeys and two deer! The daily bag limit for geese in the September season was eight! In some areas of Maine, game animal populations are at oppressive and unhealthy levels because we have fewer hunters and a lot of land that is closed to hunting.

I was born a Maine hunter and the true blessing of each deer season is that I still enjoy it with my dad, Ezra Smith. If it's possible, Dad is a more hardcore hunter than I am.

Opening day brought heavy rain and I decided to sleep in. That wasn't the case with Dad. About 7:30 a.m. Linda heard someone shoot down near Dad's stand and got me up to check on it. I put on my rain gear and trudged down there.

It was a deluge, but Dad was sitting under a huge blue umbrella, in a comfortable chair, enjoying his coffee and having what he described as a "great morning!" He'd neither seen nor shot at a deer. So I plead genetics to explain my own hunting obsession.

Describing to nonhunters why and how we hunt is tough. It goes something like this. Dad and I paddle down Hopkins Stream on a sparkling cold morning. Buffleheads take to the air ahead of us as we focus on the shoreline hoping to spot a deer. Anticipation is the greatest part of hunting.

Dad climbs into a nice two-man ladder stand that I bought for him two years ago. I choose to walk my woodlot. Two moose are spotted but no deer this morning, another "great morning" for both of us. We paddle back downstream, very satisfied with our hunt.

On another cool morning, I explore the magnificent Kennebec Highlands with Dad, Ed, and his son Jimmy. Each deer season I try to select one new area to explore. This year was special as I trudged around both the Highlands and a gorgeous piece of forest in Readfield village's shotgun-only area. I didn't shoot a deer in either place, though.

So we moved into the muzzleloading season with great anticipation, still possessing that bonus doe permit. And finally, we had snow! There is great excitement in tracking deer in the snow. We had the woods to ourselves.

And boy, did we see deer! Following a fresh track through my bog, I jumped four deer out of their beds and quickly began tracking one of them through the thick brush. Little did I know that they'd only gone about 20 yards and stood there waiting to see what was coming.

Intent on the tracks I was following, I jumped when a deer snorted at me, and I turned to see a large deer leaping away into the bushes, just 20 feet away. No shot, but I did have a big smile on my face.

As the setting sun brushed the tops of my hemlocks on the final afternoon, I sat above them on a high ridge, grateful for the snowy decorations on the trees. God truly blessed me this hunting season, even though I never used my doe permit and put no venison in the freezer.

And that, my friends, is hunting.

Walking and talking and killing a deer

Yes, you can walk and talk and still getcha deer. A friend and I were walking a tote road near my house, heading out of the woods for lunch and chatting up a storm when a huge buck jumped up about 40 yards to our right. My friend unloaded his rifle, five shots, as the buck ran through the woods and crossed the road about 125 yards in front of us.

I didn't think my friend had hit the buck, as it disappeared in the woods ahead of us. But then I looked up to the left and there he was, standing broadside to us on a knoll and glancing our way. I raised my rifle, got him in the scope, shot once, and down he dropped. My friend insisted that he'd hit the buck, but when we checked the deer over closely, there was only one bullet hole, and it was mine.

Not far from there one other day, I was sitting behind a huge downed tree with my young nephew, Nate Damm, who was not yet hunting but wanted to spend the day with me. My Dad was hunting down below us, along the stream, and we were watching a deer trail, hoping Dad would push one our way.

Nate was the first to spot the large doe as it emerged from a thicket, trotting along on the trail and heading right for us. "Well Nate," I said, "She looks like a good deer. It is getting late in the season and I haven't gotten a deer yet."

The doe was now halfway to us and I continued, "What do you think? I do have a doe permit. Should I shoot her?"

"Yea, I think so," he replied. "She's big."

And she was, and she was getting close to us. She was about 20 yards away, still with no idea we were there, hidden behind the downed tree, when I quickly raised my rifle and said, "OK Nate, I think I will." And I did. She dropped nearly at our feet.

Another interesting hunt happened just a few hundred yards from that spot. It was the first day of the season and I was casually walking an old abandoned woods road when I crested a knoll and spotted a buck on the top of the wooded hill to my right, over toward the stream.

I ducked behind a tree and watched the buck, which turned in my direction, then disappeared. I couldn't imagine where he'd gone, but soon he appeared again, standing tall and headed right for me. He got to within 35 yards, and as he got even with me, I shot him. He took three steps and dropped, a nice 8-pointer.

Later, trying to figure out why he had disappeared, I suspected that he'd gotten down on his knees and crawled under a downed tree, rather than walk around it!

Driving deer to distraction

Sometimes, small changes in hunting laws bring big benefits. One year, my big buck was the result of a small law change that was proposed by the Sportsman's Alliance of Maine. It legalized deer driving by groups of no more than three hunters, as long as noisemakers were not used.

The deer-driving statute had been so strict that it prohibited even two hunters from planning and implementing a hunt in which one hunter tried to move deer toward a second hunter. Many Mainers hunt together this way, but technically they were violating the law.

On Friday morning, November 3, I loaded my new Browning BAR Mark II semi-auto 30-06 Springfield rifle in my kitchen and walked out into a breaking dawn. I had purchased the rifle at Audette's Hardware in Winthrop the day before the firearms season on deer opened after my Remington Woodmaster failed to fire when I tried to sight it in.

In a rush to take the new gun home and sight it in so it would be ready the next morning when the season opened, I was some old mad when I failed the required FBI background check. Please be assured that I am not prohibited from owning firearms. But for some reason, even though my Social Security number was provided, the FBI "delayed" the approval of the sale of the gun to me. So I had to leave it at Audette's.

Perhaps everyone was on coffee break when Audette's called FBI headquarters in New Jersey. Who knows? The FBI doesn't have to provide any reason for a delay in approval. The "instant check" can actually take three days – that's the federal definition of "instant!"

I used my son's rifle to start the season and was finally able to pick up my new rifle the following Tuesday after the FBI decided it was OK for me to purchase a new gun. Thank you very much.

As I approached my stand, I was toting the new Browning on that Friday morning, the end of the first week of the 2000 season. The ground blind selected for the morning's hunt was a short walk from my house. Settling into my ground blind overlooking an active buck scrape, my mind was on previous successful hunts at this spot that produced deer for three generations of Smiths—my dad Ezra, my son Joshua, and me.

Hot coffee and fresh cranberry muffins provided an enjoyable experience, even though no deer joined me for breakfast. At 7:30 a.m., Dad hunted down through the woods hoping to move a deer toward me. No luck, at least not initially.

Time to try a different area. Now that it is legal, we can plan our hunt and work together with clear consciences. I won't say we'd never done it before, but now we were legal!

Previous week's hunt

A planned hunt three days earlier almost resulted in a small buck for Dad. About 8 a.m., he dropped me off about a mile from my house and drove to an old tote road nearby. While he was walking into his stand near the edge of a small pond, I sat and enjoyed a beautiful view of the pond and surrounding hills. I gave him a half-hour before starting my drive.

Sauntering in a zigzag pattern through thick spruce and cedar, it wasn't until I got to the far side of this patch of woods that I jumped a deer in a small clearing. It was bedded under a downed pine tree amid thick raspberry bushes. I saw just the silhouette of the deer as it rose from its bed, and I noticed a decent rack of antlers. It stayed below the raspberries, not offering me a shot until finally it left the clearing and entered the woods. As it did so, I got off one decent shot, a clean miss. Later, I would be grateful for that miss.

The soft ground allowed me to note that the deer headed toward Dad, but I didn't need to track him because about two minutes later I heard Dad shoot. Our plan had worked! I had jumped a deer and moved it to Dad. I raced along eager to see if we had a deer down. No such luck. Dad scored a clean miss, just like me. But I was pleased that I had missed when Dad told me the buck was small, not something I wanted to shoot the first week of the season – maybe later, but not yet. We both had any-deer permits but did not plan to use them until we were desperate near the end of the season.

Bigger buck

Later, we got a chance at a much bigger buck. On that first Friday morning after Dad arrived at my stand, we worked out a plan. Dad moved to a stand at the edge of the bog that overlooked a deer trail, while I circled around him, trying to move something his way.

Crossing a meadow of wild grass that was left when a beaver dam went out, I heard a couple of deer in an oak grove up ahead. This five-acre grove features tall acorn-producing oaks in a thicket of spruce and pine. I often jump deer here. But the situation offered no chance on this day to quietly sneak up to the deer. I hunkered down, hoping they'd appear in the meadow and give me a shot.

Gradually, I crept closer and closer. Eventually, nearing the end of the meadow, I approached within 30 yards of one deer. It was just on the other side of some thick spruce trees, making quite a racket as it pawed up acorns. I strained to see even a small part of the deer, but no such luck. I could still hear the other deer too, farther ahead in the oak stand. But I never saw either deer. Eventually, they wandered off.

I moved through the area, trying to push the deer back toward Dad, but couldn't find them. I knew they hadn't gone far so I returned to Dad's stand. We discussed a plan, deciding I would swing behind the deer while Dad circled them to take a stand about a quarter-mile away along a brook where we thought they would run if I jumped them. A bedding area was between us and that's where I expected to find the deer.

It was a good plan but things didn't work out exactly according to our hopes – not unusual when hunting whitetail deer. Anyone who thinks two or three hunters can effectively drive deer with any degree of confidence and consistency is wrong. Nine out of ten times, even the best plans fail. Our plan this day didn't fail, it just didn't work the way we anticipated.

We had just split up. Dad headed north up and over a ridge and down toward the brook, while I headed south to crest that same ridge and swing in behind the deer to move them toward Dad. I planned to stop on the ridge to give him time to get to his stand. Then I would move through the bedding area.

Surprise! As I crested the ridge, I heard a deer blow twice somewhere between Dad and me. We had only split up about ten minutes earlier and Dad wasn't more than a couple hundred yards away. I didn't know if the deer was blowing at me or at Dad.

Well, it turned out the deer had spotted Dad. That blowing deer brought me to attention and got the adrenalin going.

Here comes the deer

I stood still next to a tall pine, looking in the direction of the deer that blew, and within seconds I saw a doe coming straight at me. I got the scope on her as she turned to her left about 40 yards in front of me. The woods are thick and there were few shooting lanes or opportunities. I had to make a quick decision. I lowered the rifle and let her go. She moved off to my right.

Seconds later on the same trail, a large rack appeared, also headed right at me. That's what I saw first – a beautiful set of antlers moving in my direction.

Snapping the rifle up, the scope showed a huge buck. But things happened quickly and there was no time for buck fever to set in – fortunately. At the same spot where the doe turned, the buck stopped and glanced the other way. For some reason, he intended to go right, where the doe went left. In a split second, I decided this was my best opportunity and fired just as the buck turned. He offered a good shoulder shot.

Bang! The new gun felt good. I glanced up, glanced left, glanced right. Where did he go? Then I saw him, on the ground flopping around. I moved up to him quickly and took a finishing shot. In a matter of seconds our deer drive – in reverse – had worked. Before me was the biggest deer I'd ever shot, with a gorgeous 8-point rack. I hollered, "Dad! We got him!"

And we had. The planned hunt – the deer drive – had worked, not as planned, but it worked nonetheless. Dad jumped the deer and pushed them back to me. I thanked him for his effort after he arrived a few minutes later.

Deer drives don't always work the way you hope – in fact, they seldom do. The key ingredients to a successful two- or three-man drive are these: Know your territory well and be familiar with the habits of the deer that live there. Once in a great while, you'll succeed, as we did. It was nice to do it legally.

At Ballard Custom Meats in Manchester, the buck weighed 214 pounds. It earned me my second "Biggest Bucks" patch in 20 years and it was one Dad and I never forgot.

Dad's big buck

Dad had a great story about a deer drive, too, but it wasn't our deer drive. One morning, Dad walked down through a neighbor's woodlot, where we had permission to hunt, and set up a couple hundred yards into the woods to watch a deer trail. I canoed downstream that morning, planning to hunt up toward Dad.

He didn't know it, but shortly after he settled in hunters from Vienna who often engaged in big deer drives arrived. They sent two groups of shooters into the woods. One group set up above Dad toward the road. The other group set up behind him toward the stream. Neither knew that Dad was stationed between them, nor did he know they were there.

A third group started the drive from the road, and soon after entering the woods they jumped a buck and doe, which ran right by the first group of shooters. All of them took shots but did not hit either deer. Dad, of course, heard the shooting, and soon after, saw the deer coming his way. The buck was really flying and Dad made one of the best shots ever. He dropped it with a single shot at about 125 yards.

The boys from Vienna were not happy! The buck was huge and when I got up to Dad, we decided to return home to get the carrier in order to get the deer out of the woods and up to the road. At the Mount Vernon Country Store, it weighed in at 238 pounds.

Of pheasants and fathers

The crisp autumn afternoon, the stiff point of the English setter, the explosion of a pheasant from the tall grass, the heft of the shotgun as I brought it to my shoulder, the crack which cut the cool air, and the folding of the colorful bird followed quickly by the dog's retrieve, set my course for a lifetime. Dad's presence right behind me reinforced the hunting tradition and all its glory.

On my office wall, I still have the photo of us with the setter and my first pheasant. I look awfully small but I must have been

12 years old. Here's the story, which I wrote for Father's Day 1986, and dedicated to dads everywhere who have memories to share, or memories in the making.

Thanks, Dad!

The young boy's head barely pushed above the tall field grass as father, son, and English setter leaped from the car. Carefully loading his shotgun, the boy looked with anticipation at the lakeside field his dad had chosen for this pheasant-hunting expedition.

Jipsy the setter was straining at the leash. She knew her job and was anxious to get started. The boy was even more anxious. It was his first year afield and the anticipation had fired his imagination for many months.

There had been days and days of shooting clay pigeons at Dad's sportsman's club range in preparation for this day. His dad had made sure the boy had taken the hunter safety course the previous fall. Dad had spent many hours since then at the range, letting the boy get in some shooting. The boy had a good eye and could shoot clay pigeons with the best of them. But firing at a fleeing bird was another story. The boy wondered how difficult it would be.

Dad was ready, finally, to proceed into the field, the setter working the edges. Jipsy quickly picked up the scent and proceeded out toward the middle of the field which slanted northerly up a steep incline. Head bobbing above the field grass, shotgun at the ready, the boy stalked carefully beside his dad, well aware of the procedures to be followed if a bird took off in front of them. Safety was his dad's middle name.

And suddenly, it happened. Forever after, even into his own middle age, the boy would remember vividly every bit of the next 60 seconds. The setter on point. The pheasant flushed out in front of them. Letting off the safety of his shotgun and taking careful aim. Wondering why his dad had not yet shot. And finally getting his own shot off.

The pheasant falling to the ground. The setter pounding up the hill to retrieve the downed bird. The boy's first pheasant. He would never forget it. Neither would his dad, who still displays in his den the photo of that pint-size boy proudly holding his first pheasant. Thanks, Dad!

Postscript: After Dad died, I found in his attic a painting he'd done of Jipsy on full point, with a photo of the same scene tucked into the corner of the frame. It brought tears to my eyes. Dad took up painting when he retired, but I can't recall ever seeing this painting. It now hangs in my office.

Forty years later

Forty years later, I returned the favor and introduced Dad to turkey hunting. After a year of hunting turkeys myself, I knew he'd love the challenge, camaraderie, and interchanges with the tom turkeys.

A couple of years ago, on opening day of the May season on turkeys, we sat at the edge of a Mount Vernon corn field as I "talked turkey" to a tom down in the woods. Eventually, the tom moved into the field and headed for our decoys. Dad shot him at about 20 yards, a hefty 21-pound bird. I retrieved the bird. We haven't had setters in a long time.

What we do have is a generational bond, forged in the fields and forests and on the lakes and rivers of Maine. Hunting and fishing have always been my links to Dad. The time we spent together in the woods and on the water is priceless – beyond the comprehension of those who are less privileged.

Another morning

The canoe paddle dips silently into the calm water of Hopkins Stream, mist hiding the shoreline ahead, allowing us to sneak up to three buffleheads that take off in surprise. A muskrat slowly meanders toward shore in no hurry to get away. He steps up on land and gazes out at us.

We quietly exit the canoe, quickly glancing at the oak knoll in front of us where deer have been feeding heavily. Fresh deer sign is everywhere as we trudge 300 yards to our ground blind on the top of a small ridge overlooking the oaks.

This morning, Dad and I choose to sit together. He looks one way, I look the other. It's quiet, comforting, cleansing for the mind and body. I've been known to nap in the woods during deer season. We enjoy coffee and muffins, content to sit in anticipation.

Anticipation that a deer may appear at any moment is the very best part of the hunt, and we do a lot of anticipating. This particular morning, that's all we do. No deer appear, although later in the morning I jump one in a thick fir stand and hear the crack and commotion of an escaping whitetail without casting my eyes on the critter.

I pause to enjoy the smell of the firs, the cushion of the mossy forest floor, the skittering of red squirrels, and the sharp taste of my fresh Maine apple. A chickadee alights two feet from my face, unafraid. I remember the time an ermine ran up my leg and arm while I sat on the ground leaning against a tree. Last year, I was mesmerized by two fishers cavorting along through my woodlot. They never saw me. You see amazing things while hunting. As I move into an open area with a parcel of standing dead trees, a magnificent pileated woodpecker cries out, then lands 30 yards away. Wow! What a bird!

I am living proof that hunting does not destroy the ability to love the critters in the forest. A few I shoot and eat, respectful of them and what they contribute to my life and my table. I am not a killer. I am a hunter. And I do understand the difference, thanks to Dad.

39

Baby Ada's deer call

My 3-month-old granddaughter, Ada Claire Smith, was wailing away on my shoulder, so I stepped out onto the second-story deck of our son Josh and daughter-in-law Kelly's home in Bridgewater, Massachusetts. I thought the change of scenery might quiet her. Unfortunately, it didn't.

As she continued to screech, I was startled when a doe deer burst out of the bushes in the woods around the back of the house. She had a look of alarm on her face and dashed to the stairs leading up to the deck. She looked up at us and snorted. I thought she was going to come right up the stairs and I'd started to back up toward the door into the house when she turned and leaped back toward the woods.

But the deer stayed on the lawn, darting all over the place, stopping suddenly here and there, pawing up the ground, looking up at us and snorting. Finally, she ran back into the woods and I took a deep breath.

Apparently, the doe took Ada's cries to be those of a fawn. That's the only explanation I could come up with. Perhaps this fall, I'll try a wailing baby call from my deer stand! Or just take Ada with me!

Bagging last year's buck – this year

I am sure it was the same deer. Last year, on the last day of the firearms season on deer, a small four-point buck wandered up to my tree stand, offering a shot at about 15 yards. I looked him over carefully, decided he would be bigger next year, remembered how much I enjoy the muzzleloading season to follow and let him pass.

Even after two misfires and one missed shot during that muzzleloading season, I never questioned the decision to let that small buck live. In fact, I had already seen more than 20 deer from that stand, a fantastic season for any deer hunter.

Yesterday afternoon, about 4 p.m., sitting in that same stand, I heard a snap in front of me I lifted my rifle, started to pay attention and saw a deer step through a small opening in the trees about 100 yards in front of me. I was pretty sure I saw antlers, but his nose was on the ground.

I knew just what he was doing and where he was going. He was on the trail of a doe, a trail that would take him right past me about 60 yards to my right. From my seat, I turned slightly to get into position while he moved through a section where I had no view of him. When he stepped into an opening, I got a good look through my scope. Medium-sized buck. Probably 150 pounds. Looked to have six or eight points.

Still unsure if I'd shoot him, I shifted my view ahead to the exact spot on the trail where I'd shot a nice buck five years ago. Soon, he walked into the scope. His head was up. Definitely eight points. At least 150 pounds. So I shot him.

He bounded ahead about 30 yards, stopped, and I shot him again. Down he went. I emptied my gun, grabbed my backpack and scampered down the ladder, hustling over to where he dropped. Nice long-bodied deer, eight points, a good one. And that's when it occurred to me that this could be the buck I passed up last year.

I remembered how, after shooting a buck from this stand two years ago in the final minutes of the hunting day, I had almost sliced off the end of my thumb while cleaning out the deer in the dark. So I got to work quickly – and carefully - before it got dark.

I completed the job. I should have gone for help – especially given my recent heart problems – but I took my time, rested often, and got him to the stream and into the canoe. I paddled back to the landing, walked home in a sweat to get the Subaru Forester, drove back, heaved him into the back and got him to the tagging station. It took about 90 minutes and I missed church choir practice.

Fortunately, I still have a few friends I can hunt with, sans rifle, because there's a lot of season still to go. I love being in the woods this time of year, anticipating the sighting of deer. At Ballard's the next morning, the buck weighed in at 152 pounds. He was definitely the one I passed up last year.

Thanksgiving bucks – got one, lost one

I've had some memorable hunts on Thanksgiving mornings before gathering with family for the annual feast. Here are two of my most memorable Thanksgiving encounters with big bucks.

An icy morning heats up

Crunch, crunch, crunch. I could hear him plodding along the frozen ground through a stand of spruce out in front of me, coming from the stream and moving to my left. But I couldn't see him. To make that much noise with each step, I thought he must be big.

Excited by a good covering of snow that Thanksgiving morning, I'd gotten out early, driven the short distance to the landing on my neighbor's property, canoed downstream, and hustled the 250 yards to a ground blind I'd constructed on the top of a small ridge overlooking a well-worn deer trail.

About 7 a.m., I heard the deer coming, but he was not on the trail that would pass by me. I stood up, still hidden by small firs, and strained to find a spot in his path where I might get a look and a shot. But he was just too far away, and moving right along. Yet I could hear every step he took. Frustrating!

Then he turned and started into a stand of small pines and spruce to my left. Many of the trees were about 10 feet or so tall and crowded so closely together that I would have no chance at him as he proceeded past me. As I gazed up into the firs, there was one open spot. If he moved through it, I might get a quick shot. So I raised my gun, rested it on a small spruce beside me, and focused the scope on that open spot.

When the buck stepped into that spot, I gasped. He was huge! And not only was he centered in my scope, but he stopped right in that spot and stood broadside, offering a perfect shot. I fired once and looked up.

He was gone. Had I missed? How could I have missed? And then I saw the firs moving wildly, as he thrashed on the ground.

Snapping on the safety of my rifle, I moved off the ridge and into the firs that were so thick that I actually had trouble finding him. And when I did, I thanked God for blessing me that morning with a very, very big buck. Even though we were at the end of the season, and he'd lost a lot of weight during the rut, he still weighed 188 pounds, with a magnificent rack. He's the buck featured in the cover shot for my outdoor news blog. The snowy scene made for very nice photos.

I hustled to clean him out because I was supposed to meet Dad back at the landing at 8 a.m. so he could join me in the morning hunt. But when I pushed off in the canoe into the stream, I saw Dad standing on the opposite bank. He turned out to be on the track of my buck, which had come down the hill on the other side of the stream, walked right past my vehicle and upstream, swam across the stream, and then walked up to me.

"You could have stayed in your vehicle and got him," said Dad. But that is not the whole story of this memorable hunt. We drove back to the house to get my teenage son Josh, because I knew I'd need help getting this buck to the stream, into the canoe, back to the landing and into the vehicle. It was no longer snowing, but the snow clung to the firs and covered the ground, offering a beautiful scene as the three of us sat near the buck, enjoying cups of coffee as I related my hunting story.

Dad had an any-deer permit that year, but hadn't used it, so he carried his rifle until we got to the buck, then leaned it up against a tree. We were chatting away when I looked over Dad's shoulder and spotted two does walking right up to us, no more than 30 feet away! All I could do was choke out, "Dad, look!"

He did, and then he bolted the 15 feet to his rifle, as we watched the does take off. Of course, they were long gone by the time he got to his gun.

It took the better part of the morning to get the big buck to the tagging station, but we did get back to the house in time to clean up and enjoy the fantastic dinner that Linda and other family members had prepared.

Boy, that turkey never tasted better!

A big disappointment on Thanksgiving morning

This Thanksgiving morning found Dad and me hunting out behind the farm where he grew up. It was clear and cold, and I sat on an overturned pail, watching a deer trail, while Dad hunted his way from the farm, through the woods, across the brook, and up the ridge to me. We'd planned a two-hour hunt.

We hunted these woods every year, to the point that I became as knowledgeable about them as Dad. I could tell him to go stand by the boulder where he shot the big doe that time, and he'd know right where I was talking about.

This was a forest of about 500 acres, giving us plenty of chance to roam. We especially loved hunting along the high ridge that followed the small meandering brook all the way through the property. Our favorite ground blind was a seat in an old abandoned car overlooking a line of apple trees still producing a crop despite being in the deep woods.

I doubted Dad would have much of a chance this particular morning, because the ground was frozen and walking was very noisy. He did plan to stop for a while on the ridge overlooking the brook, so that would be his best chance. I don't really like to sit, so I would occasionally get up and wander off to my left, making a small swing around until I got warmed up and back to my seat.

About 90 minutes had gone by when, having just sat down again, I heard the deer coming up the hill. Each step on the frozen ground sounded like a cannon going off. The deer was headed right for me on the trail I was watching and would pass by about 50 yards away. I had picked an opening in the small firs for my shot, so I got the rifle up to my shoulder, getting ready for the shot while I gazed to the left to see if I could get a glimpse.

That might have been my mistake, because when I saw the huge rack, I started shaking. And when the big buck got to my opening, I shot and missed. He didn't seem all that concerned, as his steady, clomp, clomp, clomp proceeded through the firs and across the woods road behind me. I raced after him, to no avail.

Linda still remembers how morose I was at the Thanksgiving table. That was a huge buck. And I'd somehow, at just 50 yards, missed him completely. Didn't even get a bit of hair. Nothing. Nada.

But like so many of our deer hunting experiences, that was not the end of the story. The next morning, another bright and sunny day but still very cold with a hard-frozen ground, Dad and I decided to try the same strategy. He would start at the farm, but this time, he was going to hunt steadily along, and get to my stand in about an hour.

I dropped him off and drove around to my spot, parking off the woods road by an old cemetery. I'd left my bucket there, but moved it about 10 yards toward the deer trail. And I sat still, not moving, for the entire hour, praying for another chance at that big buck, but knowing that prayers are not always answered, especially when they were as selfish as mine!

About the time I expected to see Dad, I heard the deer coming. Each step toward me ratcheted my heart beat up another notch. I raised my rifle, aiming at the same spot where I'd missed the day before - but now I was only about 40 yards away.

I nearly missed my chance when the buck stepped into that opening. I was stunned. It was the same deer! The one I'd missed! He was back! This time I hit him solidly and he jumped forward, giving me a second shot. And then something happened that I'd never seen before.

The buck raced about 20 yards up hill, ran headfirst into a tree, and flipped completely upside down before crashing to the ground.

Dad was still a couple hundred yards away but said he could hear me yelling. Yep. I was some old excited!

This buck was a 9-pointer, 186 pounds! My prayers had been answered! Dad mounted the head and placed it in his living room, right next to the first big buck he ever shot, in 1947.

One scrape, three deer

I love to hunt ground scrapes that bucks use to mark their territory. Across Route 41 from my house, I found a line of scrapes one season made by a buck after he emerged from the nearby bog. I lugged over a seat and placed it in a fir thicket, about 50 yards from the scrape. I vowed to sit there until the buck arrived.

On the second day of the season, I sent Dad down to sit in the blind while I hunted down over a hill and through the bog in his direction. About 8:00 a.m., I heard him shoot and, after a brief pause, shoot again. Well, a spikehorn had emerged from the bog, trotted up toward the scrape, and Dad had shot him. But before Dad could even get out of his seat, a big buck came along behind the spikehorn, and Dad took a shot at him, a clean miss.

Now I was sold on that spot, so for the next few mornings I crawled out of bed in the darkness and sneaked over to that blind, sitting there for several hours. One morning, after I had incorrectly set my alarm, I jumped out of bed when it went off, dressed quickly, tossed some food and a novel into my backpack, grabbed my rifle, and trudged over to the blind. It seemed awfully dark when I got there, so I checked my watch. It was 4:00 a.m., an hour and a half before legal shooting time. I'd gotten up an hour earlier than I intended!

Well, there was nothing to do but sit there and that's what I did. At 7:00 a.m. I was reading the novel when I looked up and that big buck was straddling the scrape. I hadn't heard him walk up. Carefully setting the book down and picking up the rifle, I poked the barrel out between the limbs of the firs in front of me and shot at him. He whirled around and took off and I shot again. And then he was gone.

After calming down, I walked out to the scrape and saw quite a bit of blood. I'd hit him hard. Walking over to where I'd shot at him a second time, I found a tine off his antler. Yes, I'd shot the tine right off his antlers! Knowing I should wait and let him settle down someplace, I raced after him anyways, jumping him twice before I decided I needed help.

Dad was expecting to meet me at the hunter's breakfast at the Vienna Grange Hall, so I hiked home and drove over there, telling Dad my exciting story and grabbing him and a friend, Ray Anderson, and headed back to the woods.

I had followed the buck to where it entered a thicket of firs, quite close to Route 41, and hoped he had lain down there. I positioned Ray and Dad on opposite sides of the thicket and followed the blood trail into the firs. Almost instantly I heard Dad shoot. Sure enough, the buck was in there and he leaped out right in front of Dad. So Dad got the first and the last shot at that buck!

Josh's deer

The story gets better. The next year, another buck was making scrapes in that same place, so I decided to continue to use that blind. My 16-year-old son Josh was sitting there with me one afternoon when we heard deer coming down over the hill behind us, headed our way.

A nice doe stepped out first, right by the scrape, and Josh calmly shot at her. She leaped forward, disappearing quickly, and we heard her tearing up over the hill to our right. I figured he had missed.

So when two more deer, another nice doe and a lamb, stepped out by the scrape, I whispered in a loud voice, "Shoot, Josh, shoot." But he didn't lift his gun and they sauntered on past us and out of view. When I asked him why he hadn't shot, he said, "Because I shot at the other deer, Dad."

And sure enough, we found the first doe, about 100 yards away, dead. And I knew immediately that my son was a better hunter than I was!

Dad's three-day deer

As the day darkened, a doe stepped out into the field at the end of my road and Dad shot it, knocking out one leg. The deer quickly turned and hobbled back into the woods before he could get off another shot, and he followed it for a bit, but gave up quickly, deciding to wait until the next day to trail it.

We both returned to that spot the next day, and trailed the deer up the hill, through a field, and down to Hopkins Stream, where we jumped it and got off a long shot, a clean miss. We tracked that deer all that day, all the way down the stream toward Kents Hill, then back again, ending up only about a quarter mile from where Dad had shot her. Twice we got a glimpse of the deer, and once we got off another shot, but we couldn't stop her.

At the end of that day, Dad was discouraged. We walked out at dusk and Dad wanted to give up, but I suggested we return to that spot the next day, and see if she'd lain down and died. So we did that, starting right where we'd left her trail, quickly finding her lying down in a fir thicket. She took off again, so I sent Dad high up on the hill and well ahead of her, gave her time to settle down, then took off after her.

Dad was stationed at the top of a clear cut and I jumped the deer on the edge of that cut. She was moving pretty slow by then, through the chopping, and I was actually catching up to her when I came to my senses, stopping so Dad could get a shot at her. And shoot her he did, finally dropping her.

Yet another demonstration of the fact that you should never give up on a wounded deer.

Maine outdoor writer enjoys her first-ever hunt

It was my privilege to introduce Maine Today Media outdoor writer Deirdre Fleming to hunting, accompanying her on her first-ever deer hunt the first week of November 2015. I'm now calling her DEERdre. Her story of our hunt, published on the front page of the Maine Sunday Telegram, was exceptionally good.

Today, I'm going to tell you the rest of the story. Well, some of the rest of the story. Let's start with a correction. Deirdre cleaned up my act a bit when she wrote that when those small deer stepped out into the field, I whispered "deer." Actually, I loudly whispered, "Shoot! Shoot!"

Deirdre impressed me with her cautious and deliberate approach to deer hunting. She wouldn't shoot at a running – or even a trotting – deer. And she wouldn't shoot at those small deer, no matter how enthusiastically I encouraged her to do so. She did some sitting, but also walked a lot with me, still hunting through the woods.

Our three days of hunting were especially memorable thanks to George and Brenda Joseph, owners of Steep Hill Farm in Fayette, the best place to pick blueberries in the state. The Josephs are good friends of mine and allow me to bring other hunters to their farm, knowing we emphasize safety. I love bringing new adult hunters and young hunters here. Last year, Harry Vanderweide's adult daughter Amanda shot her first deer here.

Deirdre's hunt

In three days of hunting at Steep Hill Farm, Deirdre and I saw 17 deer. When neither of us got an any-deer permit in the lottery, I sought a friend who would transfer a permit to her. I knew it would give her a much better chance of getting a deer, and the Josephs really wanted some does shot this year. Angus King III, the son of our U.S. senator, stepped up and transferred his permit in our District 16 to Deirdre.

On the third afternoon, we took a seat on the edge of a field and sat for the final two hours of the hunting day. We'd only been sitting for about 20 minutes when a small doe stepped out into the field about 100 yards away. I can't imagine any other first-time hunter passing up that shot, but Deirdre did, judging the deer too small.

Shortly after that, a big doe appeared in the woods to our right, headed toward the field. Deirdre watched it approach, and by the time she was comfortable shooting, she had to lean to the right from her seat and shoot at the deer as it stood between two trees. She missed.

The deer leaped into the field and stood about 60 yards away, unsure where the shot had come from. And that's when Deirdre jumped up to prepare a second shot. The doe saw her and took off back toward the woods. Deirdre's shot passed behind the deer. She didn't seem too disappointed. She did say that we probably wouldn't see any other deer, now that she'd shot a couple of times. But I knew that was not the case because there was more than an hour left and there were a lot of deer here.

That's when she told me she was a far better shot standing up. I'd had her sitting behind a stone wall. And while I was not happy to see her standing, fearing she was too visible, I have to admit it worked out well.

About 20 minutes after she'd shot, another doe stepped out into the field. Yes, this is an amazing place to hunt! While I was urging her to shoot, in an ever-louder voice, her head was waving no, no, no. Finally she turned and whispered to me that it was too small. "It's a nice deer," I told her. But apparently not nice enough for my very selective hunter!

Just after sunset, with about 25 minutes left to hunt, a group of four deer trotted up over the ridge to an apple tree in the field about 120 yards away. I discovered later that three other deer were with them but didn't come up over the ridge. I glanced at Deirdre and knew I didn't have to encourage her to shoot. She looked pretty calm, actually, and had her gun up and ready. She had to wait briefly for the deer to divide, or she might have hit two with a single shot. When the deer did split up, she selected the biggest doe and shot it.

As it limped our way, she glanced at me. I think she might have been hoping I'd shoot, but I told her to get ready for another shot, and when the deer got about half way to us, she made a nice shot in the forward shoulder and dropped it.

George Joseph came out to congratulate her and I didn't make her clean the deer. She said she'd like me to teach her to do that, but I'm not sure she was watching too closely! We took the deer over to Fike's Custom Cutting in Readfield, where Brandon and his family do a super job of cutting up domestic and game animals. Tomorrow I've got to get over there and pick up the ten pounds of venison that Deirdre generously donated to our Mount Vernon food bank.

As we drove over to Fike's, after registering the deer at the Fayette Country Store, I told Deirdre deer hunting would never be that easy again. We spoiled her!

Hunting has changed a lot in my lifetime

Introducing a segment on the end of the firearms season on deer, the female TV newscaster issued a warning that "some of the images might be disturbing." My, how hunting has changed in my lifetime. We would mount our dead deer on the front hood of the car and parade up Winthrop's Main Street, then hang the deer in the front yard for all to see and admire. Yes, admire. I don't believe anyone found the dead deer to be disturbing.

As the TV segment was showing, I was wondering if people who pass the supermarket meat counters are disturbed by all that meat, cut out of animals for their dining pleasure. Can it really be disturbing to see a deer killed by a hunter who values the opportunity to harvest his or her own animals and feed his or her family fresh, healthy meat?

I realize that a lot has changed for hunters since I began hunting 55 years ago, some for the good, some not so good. On

51

the good side, hunters today are much more attuned to conservation and actually pay for all of the good work of the Department of Inland Fisheries and Wildlife on behalf of the wild critters all Mainers enjoy seeing. The epidemic of "No Trespassing" signs on private land has been one dramatically negative change, but that has forced hunters to practice good landowner relations in order to have places to hunt, and that's a very good thing.

For the second consecutive year, I chose not to shoot a deer, mostly because I get more pleasure these days out of taking others hunting, particularly new hunters. I actually posted my land this year so a local family could hunt it, along with my guests, without being disturbed by other hunters, and their 17-year-old son shot the big 8-point 185-pound buck there. He was so excited! And so was I.

I've shot deer nearly every year for the last four decades and have five big buck mounts on my office wall, another reason I am no longer driven to kill a deer every year. And the fact that Dad is gone and no longer hunting with me probably has something to do with this too. He was so proud every time I shot a deer and I never wanted to disappoint him. I wore a piece of Dad's clothing whenever I hunted this year, so in a way, he is still hunting with me.

A report from Responsive Management, the national firm headed by Mark Duda, has done research all across the country on public attitudes toward hunting and hunters. "Americans' approval of hunting has remained consistently high over nearly two decades that Responsive Management has tracked the issue," he reports. "A scientific telephone survey conducted recently found that 77% of American adults strongly or moderately approve of hunting."

More troubling is the finding that "support for hunting is conditional rather than absolute." Approval varies significantly, from 40% to 78%, depending on species, motivation, and method of hunting. At least 75% approve of deer and wild turkey hunting, but less than half approve of hunting for black bear, mountain lion, or mourning dove.

When it comes to our motivation for hunting, Duda's report continues: "American adults overwhelmingly approve of hunting for the meat (85% of all respondents expressed strong or moderate approval), to protect humans from harm (85%), for animal population control (83%), for wildlife management (81%), or to protect property (71%). However, approval diminishes fairly considerably when respondents are asked about hunting for sport (53% approve), to supplement income (44%), for the challenge (40%), or for a trophy (28%)."

Responsive Management also found that "attitudes change as people gain direct experience" with hunting. No real surprise there. For example, people in rural areas are more supportive of hunting than folks who live in urban areas, men are more supportive than women, and older folks are more supportive than young people.

The best news is that "any prevailing negative attitudes toward hunting may be mitigated through the positive impacts of mentoring experiences and strong social connections." I can tell you from firsthand experience that this is correct. My three days of hunting with outdoor writer Deirdre Fleming, who had never hunted before, turned her into a very enthusiastic hunter. I am sure Deirdre was not disturbed by that TV video!

"My" doe was killed crossing the road

A total of 46,120 deer have been killed on Maine's roadways from 2001 through 2014. And despite the fact that the deer population decreased significantly a few years ago, the total number of collisions in 2014 was the highest number in that entire 14-year period: 4,414. In that time period there were 6 fatalities, 75 incapacitating injuries, 614 other injuries, and 860 possible injuries, from collisions with deer. In 1986, I wrote the following story that brings these statistics to life.

My doe

She was crossing the road nearly every night to paw up the deep snow under the apple tree on our front lawn, trying to stave off the ravages of a tough winter with some of those red delicious apples lying frozen in their snowy grave. She was as beautiful as only a deer can be, fat and pregnant with twins.

One snowy Saturday night as I was driving the baby sitter to our house, the doe was standing on the right side of the road as I crossed the bridge over Hopkins Stream beside our house. Turning quickly she bounded into the center of the road and stopped, frozen by my headlights.

As I jammed the brake to the floor, we caught a patch of ice and skidded to the right. Working the steering wheel and brake pedal feverishly, I took our vehicle through a series of left, right, left, right skids. When we finally stopped, the doe was still standing, about three feet in front of us. A miracle had spared her life and the agony which would have stayed with me for a long time if I had hit her.

To make her life easier, I started placing apples out under the tree on top of the snow. She would gobble up the entire pile, then dig for more. Moving up our driveway with those graceful and dainty steps, she often threw caution to the wintry wind and paraded around as we admired her from the kitchen window.

One early morning as I stumbled out through the cold sub-zero dawn to collect the newspaper from its roadside delivery box, the huge red wet stain on the road beside the delivery box told a sad tale. I took in a deep gulp of that cold morning air and it stuck in my chest like a sharp knife. The blood stain was six feet in length, filled with those soft brown hairs which could only have come from our doe. Pieces of a truck's grill were scattered along both sides of the road for nearly 50 feet.

As she bounded across the road for our apple treats, the driver must have hit her broadside. I nearly cried right there in the road as I knelt beside the stain which my dog was now eagerly examining. That doe was a member of our family with a

54

connection to us that we could feel as she stared up at us standing behind the kitchen window. And now she – and her twins – were dead.

Oh, I know it happens – a lot. I've had over ten near-misses of my own – once when I passed between two deer standing in the road with only inches to spare on either side – but every deer killed by a motor vehicle, every handsome buck or pregnant doe run down by dogs or coyotes, every one taken by a poacher – grieves each and every one of us. More so when it happens in front of your home.

The blood stains washed away in the January rains. But that doe's memory remains and I stand sometimes at the kitchen window, seeing her ephemeral ghost on the evening air. A beautiful creature.

2015 postscript

In 2015 we had the biggest crop of apples on our scattering of trees around our house that we'd had in the 37 years we'd lived here. We harvested lots of apples, gave some to friends, neighbors, and the local food bank, and Linda made tons of applesauce. And the apples that we didn't harvest got gobbled up by a bunch of deer, including a large spike horn that we enjoyed watching several evenings a week from our kitchen window. There are no apples left on the trees or the ground, so all "my" deer made it safely through the apple-eating season.

Moose memories on the loose

I participated in the September moose hunt with Paul Jacques and Ed Pineau. Most know Paul for his long legislative career and service as Deputy DIF&W Commissioner. Ed and I do a lot of hunting and fishing together, and he and his wife Cate are lobbyists who lobbied for the Sportsman's Alliance of Maine when I served as SAM's executive director.

Paul's sub-permittee was unable to participate in the hunt, so he asked Ed to be his sub. Lucky Ed! Although, I fully expect Paul will shoot the bull moose. Paul's been on moose hunts every year, but this is the first time he has won his own permit. It's also the first time I have participated in a September moose hunt, when you can call in the bulls, and I am excited.

Having never been drawn for a permit (I was convinced for years that someone at DIF&W was pulling my name before the drawing because the agency was aggravated with me), I was really excited when I got a letter in August informing me that my name had been drawn as the 153rd alternate in this year's lottery - and was told it was very likely I would get a permit.

But then came the bad news. My permit would be in one of the central Maine or coastal districts. And that's what happened. When I got the call, giving me the district numbers where I could have a permit, they were not districts where I really wanted to hunt moose. But I did note that Ed and Cate Pineau live in one of the districts where I could have a permit. Seeing as how Ed is my sub-permittee, I called and asked if he'd like to shoot a moose in his backyard. I was some old relieved when he said no! And I turned down the permit.

I don't really care about shooting a moose, but I love participating in the moose hunt. Two years ago I participated in a moose hunt and wrote a four-part story about it. If you would like to read that story, here it is.

Moose Hunting Requires Endurance!
Day One of my 2012 Moose Hunt
The allure of a Maine moose hunt is difficult to convey. Sitting in the open back end of a pick-up, pitch black, 26 degrees, listening to the sounds of trees cracking in the cold, Mike Pineau trying to call in a big bull. I guess you had to be there.

In October I enjoyed my first-ever moose hunt, with Ed and Cate Pineau, Mike Pineau, Norm Pineau, Lester Pineau (partial Pineau list - there were a lot of Pineaus in camp) and our friend Kevin Stewart from Texas – the man with the permit for a bull moose in WMD 4, the location of the Pineau's camp in Northeast Carry on Moosehead Lake.

On Day One moose hunting is more about endurance, less about enjoyment. We drove over 1000 miles – at least it seemed like it. Back and forth across "unimproved" woods roads, eyes straining to see a moose. Any moose. Anywhere. It was warm. Moose were not moving. At least, that's what Maine Guide Mike Pineau told me. As far as I could tell, moose were not there, period.

Other than hearing a single grunt from a bull moose when we got out of the truck this very-early morning, we saw and heard nothing. We did see a mouse – but the slight change of an "o" for a "u" makes quite a difference.

I have very sad news to report. All the wild critters have been eradicated from the north woods – no lynx, no bobcats, no foxes, no coyotes, no deer, and certainly no moose. We did see a lot of grouse – but Ed wouldn't let me bring my shotgun and shoot them. We were moose hunting and only moose hunting.

As we drove, and drove, and drove, I snacked, and snacked, and snacked, and napped, and read a 2-day-old newspaper – and occasionally got up into the Moose Ridah attached to the truck bed, gazing out into the cuttings for those nonexistent moose as we motored along, and along, and along.

But the experience really improved when we finally got back to camp to enjoy an outstanding dinner of moose chili and moose shepherd's pie. I had three bowls of chili, one plate of shepherd's pie, and two cold beers. By 8:00 p.m. I was in bed, dead to the world. Dreaming of moose.

UP NEXT – My entire moose hunting experience was transformed on Day Two, when Norm's voice blasted from Ed's walkie talkie: "Fifty-pointer. Number seven road!"

Electrified by the Bellow of a Bull Moose
Day Two at Northeast Carry

I am freezing in the back of the Moose Ridah. We're parked at an intersection of two woods roads. It's pitch black, before the crack of dawn, nothing moving, eerily quiet, when from somewhere in Ed Pineau's pants I hear, "50-pointer! Number 7 Road!"

Ed wildly searched his various pants pockets, trying to find the walkie-talkie that had just broadcast his brother Norm's voice. Ed didn't hear what

Norm had said, so I repeated it in a shout: "That was Norm! He's seen a biggggg moose! 50-inch rack! On Number 7 road!"

And with that, I leaped out of the back of the truck and sprinted up the road where Mike Pineau and Kevin Stewart were sitting, trying to call in a bull. We quickly gathered in the truck and sped off for Number 7 road where Norm was posted.

When we arrived, Norm was standing in the road, pointing into the woods. A group of hunters around the corner had shot a small bull, and shortly after that, Norm spotted a huge bull crossing the road.

Mike started calling and immediately, just 100 yards into the woods, a bull bellowed. Oh my God! He's coming for us! It was electrifying! And suddenly I got it – the excitement, the anticipation, the adrenalin, the amazing experience that is moose hunting in Maine.

Preparation

The Pineau boys have taken 27 moose from their Northeast Carry camp, so they've got this down to a routine. This is a major project, requiring lots of equipment including saws, come-alongs, chains, a lot of rope and much more, many days spent scouting the area, a snowmobile trailer for transporting the moose, the Moose Ridah hoisted onto the back of the pickup, a butcher shop standing by in Livermore Falls – and enough food to sustain the group for six days, if necessary.

And it almost was. That big bull on Day Two bellowed once and left the area. So it was back in the truck for another day of riding the roads. But now, they couldn't keep me out of the Moose Ridah. I was pumped!

Usually one other guy would join me in the Ridah, and we spent much of the time sharing stories while staying alert for moose sightings. Many of mine turned out to be very large dark stumps. But occasionally today, we did see moose. That's when it was my job to pull on the rope that dangled down from the Ridah and through the driver's window. When I pulled, the driver stopped. Quickly. Hang on!

Mike told me that before they built the Ridah, he rode on the tailgate, watching for moose and trying desperately not to fall off. Glad I missed those hunts!

As we ride the roads, Ed or Mike, in the Ridah with me, would point out, "We got a moose right here once," and "Here's where we got a nice bull three years ago." Very impressive, especially when I was on my first moose hunt.

Near the top of a hill, I heard a loud snap, told Mike, and he pulled the rope, bringing the truck to a fast halt. Ed and Kevin jumped out of the truck, and I pointed up into the woods, where I'd heard the snap.

Mike and I jumped out of the Ridah, and I walked up the road a ways with Kevin while Ed and Mike walked the other way. A few minutes later, I heard Mike making his cow call – from up in the woods. I was amazed that he got up there so fast – until I turned to my left and saw him standing a couple hundred yards away in the road. It was the moose that was calling! And my gosh, she sounded just like Mike!

That call helped the guys decide the moose was a cow, but we stuck it out there for a while, hoping she was with a bull. The moose stayed put up on the ridge. But it was exciting!

We spent a lot of today on high ground, where the views are jaw dropping gorgeous panoramas of mountains, lakes, and foliage at its peak of reds and yellows. We also saw a Golden eagle, some kind of owl, a lot of Canadian jays, spruce grouse, and what seemed like thousands of juncos – plus more Ruffed grouse that the guys would not let me shoot. Not until we got our moose.

But there was no moose today – except in the evening's meal featuring moose meatloaf. Very very tasty. I also enjoy a couple of ice cold (left outside) Shipyards – respecting the Pineau's sound requirement that no alcohol is consumed until the day's hunt is concluded.

Up next: Day Three – Finally, I get to shoot some grouse.

Good Grouse Almighty! Moose Hunting's Exciting!
Day Three of our 2012 Moose Hunt

I awaken to the smells of bacon and coffee and the sound of a crackling fire. This is my idea of hunting camp. Norm is the breakfast chef and he even cooks our eggs to order. Superb!

Conversations in hunting camp are always interesting. We covered, of course, previous hunting and fishing adventures. We also argued politics, and *lamented the Red Sox. The talk was often brutally honest, with no egos present. If you can't stand ridicule, hunting camp is not for you.*

Before we hit the roads again this morning in search of a huge bull moose, we engage in a conversation about "malicious compliance," which means doing something that you are ordered or required to do, when you know it's the wrong thing. That will be the subject of my editorial page column in the Kennebec Journal and Waterville Morning Sentinel sometime soon!

It had rained hard the night before and I thought, as I climbed up into the Ridah before dawn, how far I'd come in two days. On the first day, with temperatures in the mid-40s, I was freezing in the Ridah and rode there for only a short time. On Day Two, when we started spotting some moose, I was happy and comfortable in the Ridah, in mid-20 temperatures.

For the last two hours today, I am alone in the Ridah, in a downpour, a big smile on my face. Everyone else is hunkered down in the truck. Every once in a while, they stopped and asked if I was ok. Of course! I loved it!

Mid-morning, I spotted a small cow up ahead in a chopping, pulled the rope, turned to my left, and was astonished to see a very large bull standing broadside, 30 yards away. Kevin was already out of the truck, taking aim, when I glanced his way. The bull stared. Kevin aimed. The bull stared some more. Kevin put down his gun. The bull continued to stare at us. And then, eventually, he wandered off.

At an estimated weight of 700 pounds, but with a relatively small rack, he was determined to be significantly short of the huge bull we were hoping to get. Ed called it "only 700 pounds" and said it was "identical to my moose last year." If I'd been the shooter, that moose would have been down, quickly. I thought he was massive! Actually, he was massive.

Finally, today, my whining about shooting grouse got to Ed and he let me give it a try. I'd noticed a grouse just off the road as we passed by. When Ed turned the truck around a couple hundred yards beyond that spot, I asked if I could get out on the way back and shoot the grouse, and he finally relented.

But I got out of the truck in the wrong place and couldn't find the grouse. Then Mike rolled down his window and told me the spot was about 75 yards up the road. I got back in the truck, road up to that spot, and saw the grouse scampering under the root of a big stump and disappearing.

Ed got out, saw the bird, and pointed it out to me, but as hard as I stared, I could not see it. "It's right there," he said about six times, pointing to the bird. Nope, couldn't see it. Finally, frustration setting in, Ed said, "Give me the gun. I'll shoot it."

"No way!" was my exclamation (or perhaps something a bit stronger). "It's right there," he nearly shouted, pointing to the stump. Thinking I saw a bit of movement to the side of the stump, I aimed at that spot and fired. Then I had to get around a lot of water in the ditch between me and the stump. And when I finally got up to the stump, I found two dead grouse. I'd gotten two birds with one shot, and didn't see either one!

"Good guiding," I told Ed, proudly holding up my two birds. I would get two more that afternoon to complete my daily limit, and returned to camp very contented, even though we didn't get a moose today. The moose roast at dinner made up for that!

It's a Cow!
Day Four of our 2012 Moose Hunt

Heavy rain, spitting snow, and a fierce wind last night got every moose in the North Woods up and moving, at least it seemed that way on the morning of Day Four of our 2012 moose hunt at Ed Pineau's Northeast Carry camp. Our shooter, Kevin Stewart of Texas, had been very patient, passing up small bulls and one I thought was massive, hoping to get a bull of more than 1000 pounds.

I started the morning in the Moose Ridah with Ed, not wanting to miss a thing. The wind was still very strong, but we started seeing moose almost immediately. Ed would spot the moose and my job would be to pull the rope, alerting the driver to stop. After an hour and a half, I was getting pretty good at pulling the rope, as we'd spotted seven moose by that time! Alas, I wasn't getting any better at spotting moose. In the early morning light, I pointed up ahead and asked Ed, "Is that a moose?"

"No," he said somewhat sarcastically. "That's a pine tree." By now, my level of excitement was so high that I was seeing moose everywhere. Most were big dark stumps. About 8:30 a.m. we were coming down a slight incline when I glanced ahead, up a tote road, and spotted what I was pretty sure was a moose. I pulled the rope, quickly stopping the truck, and brought up my binoculars. Ed was in the Ridah with me.

I pointed out the moose to Ed, quite a ways up the tote road to our left, as Kevin and Mike exited the truck and moved quickly up the road, getting into position where they could see and shoot up the tote road. There were trees and leaves between Ed and I in the Ridah and the moose, but I thought it was a cow. And here's how that went.

"It's a cow." Bang! Literally milliseconds after I said the word cow, Kevin shot. I won't tell you what Ed said next about my ability to identify moose. Very unkind! It was a huge bull, slightly larger than the one we'd seen previously, and by far the biggest we'd seen this morning: 717 pounds with a 40-inch rack. Everyone was happy.

Then the work began, although the Pineaus have this down to a science, saws, knives, rope, pulleys, and before I knew it, the bull was on the snowmobile trailer and we were headed to Raymond's Store in Northeast Carry to register the animal.

Norm had the best comment after we got back to camp. We were all standing around the trailer admiring the moose. "That's next year's menu, sitting on that trailer," said Norm. I can't wait!

Postscript

Having gotten our moose early in the day, I was able to get in some grouse hunting in the afternoon. We all piled in the truck and hit the road, looking for grouse. I shot appallingly poorly, whenever the guys would let me out of the truck to try my luck. I blamed it on the audience.

So after we got back to camp, Mike took pity on me and drove me up and into the hills behind camp. I never missed a shot, getting my limit fairly quickly. That got me some bragging rights back at camp, and allowed me to return home with my possession limit of eight grouse.

But what I really brought home was a basket load of memories of a very exciting hunt, great friends, and delicious food, along with a new-found appreciation for moose hunting in Maine. It's been years since I applied for a moose permit. But I'll be doing that in 2013!

Killing the moose was the easiest part of the hunt

At moose/deer/and grouse camp, it all starts with breakfast, the eggs and bacon sizzling, the stories flying, the laughing and (sometimes) lying going on and on. But then, it's time to get serious and hit the road. At moose camp in October, we had to leave the camp at 4:30 a.m. for an hour and a half ride to the hunting district to our north where Scott Ireland had won a permit in the June lottery. Scott's friend Greg James was his sub-permittee.

We were upta camp in Northeast Carry with Ed and Mike Pineau and their Uncle Lester, whom we call the Doctor of Deer. Boy, you should hear Uncle Lester's hunting stories! The Pineau's camp sits right on the shore of Moosehead Lake, with millions of acres of the north Maine woods in their backyard. In other words, hunting heaven. Well, heaven on this trip turned, briefly, into hunting hell. But before we get to the hunt in which I participated, let's go back a couple of weeks to the Pineau's September hunt.

The bog

Norm Pineau had the moose permit for the September hunt and Ed was his sub-permittee. Cousin Mike Pineau was along to help. And boy, was that a good thing. Uncle Lester, Ray Pineau, and Paul Jacques didn't go with them that day because it was raining. Well, it was actually the deluge we endured the last day of September.

They drove up to their designated hunting zone, and by 9:00 a.m. they'd spotted a nice bull down in a chopping. Ed and Norm shot at the beast and it ran back down through the chopping and into a bog. And the fun was over. The dream of shooting a nice bull moose turned into the nightmare of trying to haul that big critter out of the bog and up the hill through deep ruts left by a skidder, lots of downed trees, and thick brush.

They hooked up the ropes, linked to two trucks on the road, and hiked all the way down into the bog to the moose. Boy, it was a brute, and it was a long way up to the road. At 4:15 p.m., after the rope had snapped three times, and hours of poking and prodding the bull up and over every obstacle, the bull was finally nearing the road. On one haul, the truck was actually yanked off the road while the trailer flipped upside down. It took quite a while to straighten that out!

They arrived at Raymond's store about 5:30 p.m., where the bull registered 700 pounds. They will swear, forever after, that down in that bog, it was at least 7000 pounds. But they were also pleased that they got it out of the bog, happy with the size of the bull, and confident that they'd never again suffer through such a difficult hunting task. Little did they know.

The bog (again)

We drove in the darkness for more than an hour, arrived at our starting point about 20 minutes before legal shooting time and waited the 20 minutes for our October moose hunt to begin. Mike and I rode in the Moose Rider, a contraption constructed by Paul Jacques, a long-time champion of Maine sportsmen and one-time legislative leader, who has a camp just down the road from the Pineaus. The Rider, which is mounted on the bed of the truck, sported two very nice chairs which Mike and I quickly settled into, expecting to ride up there all day as the truck proceeded very slowly up the roads, searching for moose.

We'd been motoring only about 15 minutes as we approached the spot where the Pineaus had experienced their moose nightmare in September. Mike was pointing to the place where his truck slid off the road and the trailer flipped over, when he said, "Wait, there's a moose!"

Actually, there were three moose off to our left in nearly the exact spot where the September moose had stood. Later, I would say that those three bulls were standing there, still laughing about the Pineau's September nightmare.

The biggest bull was broadside, standing there looking at us, so Mike quickly pulled the rope that draped down over the windshield and signaled to Scott, who was driving the truck, that we'd seen a moose. Scott stopped, jumped out, and quickly loaded his rifle and mounted it on a tripod. But from the ground, he couldn't see the moose!

He shifted slightly to the left and spotted all three moose, but they had started to move away from us and were lined up in a row. Scott feared he would shoot more than one, so he waited. Eventually the biggest bull moved to the right giving Scott a clear shot. And he fired.

Just before he fired, Mike was on the radio to Ed and Lester, who had stayed back at the bottom of the hill in Ed's truck. "You won't believe this," said Mike, "but there are moose in the exact same spot." By the time Ed and Lester pulled up to our truck, Scott and Greg were headed down through the chopping to look for Scott's moose. It took a few minutes but when we heard him holler, we knew the moose was down. It had gone only about 15 feet, dropping in a thicket.

And that's when the nightmare began. We would have never guessed that it would take seven long and tedious hours to get that bull up to the road. Ten times it got hung up and the rope broke, often snapping so loudly it sounded like an explosion. We all stood well away from the rope so as not to get injured. At one point, the rope broke in two places at once, and the top half of the rope flew up the road and right past Lester and me. We'd actually been standing in that spot until Lester moved to the side of the road to sit, and I joined him. Otherwise that rope would have knocked us down.

Despite the difficulties, Mike, who was in charge and well-experienced, never got discouraged, simply repairing the rope and trying again. Scott and Greg stayed down in the chopping with the moose and did what they could to keep it moving. Eventually Ed wandered down into the chopping and sawed down a small tree that we would use to leverage the moose up and over the deep ruts. The chopping was full of downed trees, thick brush, deep ruts, and piles of dirt. As the afternoon arrived, it was getting hot, and we discussed various alternatives, finally deciding to double up the rope and use a come-along to ease the moose forward in the toughest spots. We also kept using Ed's leveraging tree trunk.

Eventually we got the moose to a place and position where Scott could clean it out and that really helped, removing a lot of weight and slimming the bull down. And finally, seven hours after we'd started, the moose began to slide quickly up through the thicket. When it arrived on the road, I cheered. But there was still plenty of work to be done, including a final cleaning of the moose, and loading it onto the trailer, then driving all the way back to Raymond's Store to register and weigh it.

The bull weighed 775 pounds with a 43-inch antler spread. A very nice bull. And an even better story – a story that gets better with each telling. Not that any of us would ever want to repeat that experience!

For the next few days, we all hunted grouse, which were scarce that year. Didn't matter. We drove and walked the highlands, enjoying magnificent views and the colorful foliage, had great meals prepared by chef Ed Pineau, and continued swapping stories and a few tall tales, all with quite a bit of ribbing. And yes, I got my share of that! Especially the day I missed shots at three grouse, one of them twice.

13 shots

On Day Three at Raymond's Store in Northeast Carry, where I stopped to get gas, Paul Jacques was registering and weighing the moose, while Ed Raymond recovered from leg surgery. Paul has a camp just a quarter mile down the road from the Pineaus.

As I exited the store, a half-dozen guys from southern Maine drove in in two vehicles, towing a big moose. The antlers sported a 51-inch spread and the bull weighed 829 pounds. Impressive. And they had a sort of nightmarish story, with a good ending.

On October 13, they had taken 13 shots at the bull, which had 13 points. But it was late in the day and the bull trotted down into a thick bog. They hunted for it well into the darkness, finally giving up. The next morning they scoured the area, which was quite a ways back from the road, anticipating a long haul and tough job getting the bull out of there. But they couldn't find it.

Discouraged, they walked back toward their vehicle, still searching, and were ecstatic when they found the bull just 25 yards from the road. Judging from our experience, I knew this was very good news indeed!

Duck hunting's a love affair with nature

You may hear gunshots in the marsh this morning. Duck hunting opened 30 minutes before sunrise.

If things went according to plan, at 6:00 a.m. this morning I was seated in a comfortable chair under overhanging alders, my natural blind alongside Hopkins Stream, a panorama of feathered friends – decoys – spread out in front of me. Here's how the hunt will go.

As the sun touched the top of Bowen Hill to the east, black ducks settled into the marsh all around me. Can't shoot them until next week, though, so I squint left and right, hoping for mallards or maybe some woodies.

The dog, a saw-grass Chesapeake Bay Retriever appropriately named Blake Hill Buddy, Blake for short, is settled down beside me, also scanning the horizon for ducks which he has dedicated his life to retrieving whenever his master is fortunate enough to knock one down.

We may see deer in the marsh, hear a cow moose calling somewhere in the woods behind us, witness a family of otter swim past hissing at our decoys, admire beaver as they busy themselves on the opposite shore, watch a heron fish for his breakfast, all the while straining our eyes to the sky, left and right, hoping to spot a flock of ducks winging our way.

Duck hunting is a specialty sport nowadays. Less than 10,000 sportsmen hunt ducks in Maine today. It is an expensive sport. Hunting licenses are of course required as well as a state duck stamp ($2.50) and a federal stamp ($15). Steel shot is expensive and the new more effective bismuth shot, just approved by federal authorities, costs even more.

Decoys don't come cheap these days and camo clothing is also a necessity, enough for every type of weather. I've got camo tee-shirts, camo flannel shirts, a camo hooded sweatshirt, camo pants, and camo hats. No, I didn't buy camo underwear.

Boots, foul weather gear (camo of course) and gloves complete the ensemble. I forked over big bucks this year for an LL Bean all-weather Gore-Tex insulated camo coat, good enough to keep me warm during the second season which goes into December locally and into January for sea ducks on the coast. Yes, I conceded that the coat cost more than my wife's wedding dress, but I wear it more often, and you've got to factor in inflation over the last 16 years we've been married.

I am hoping we'll still be married after the duck season, although I swing almost immediately into deer season and that's enough to strain any marriage. When the first duck season ends on October 14, I'll have just two weeks of scouting before the four weeks of the regular firearms season on deer begins, followed by (and I haven't dared tell my wife about this yet), a newly established two-week muzzle-loading season on deer. Fortunately, that ends before Christmas.

If I take up muzzle-loading, I'll need a new firearm, and that's another story. Bad enough what this duck hunting does to the pocketbook. Along with the other stuff, a canoe is necessary too, tote bags for all the gear and decoys, and duck calls. Then there is the four-wheel drive vehicle, absolutely necessary.

OK. So what if I've invested about $35,000 so far, including this new camo folding chair in which I am comfortably ensconced. It's a great sport. Worth every penny.

Conservationists are born in duck blinds. We put the resource first, reducing bag limits whenever necessary, putting up millions of dollars through Ducks Unlimited and other organizations to purchase and manage waterfowl habitat, constructing and caring for duck houses spread through the marshlands of Maine.

This year we'll bypass black ducks the first week so they can continue to rebuild their numbers. We'll have no goose season at all, as those magnificent birds struggle to overcome a serious nesting problem in the Ungava Bay Region of Canada back in 1992. But we'll be out there, no matter what the weather, because we love ducks and duck hunting. What's not to love?

Imagine yourself this morning, seated alongside me on Hopkins Stream. Hardwood trees sporting glorious red and yellow leaves reflect in the water and stand guard along both sides of the stream. The setting is gorgeous. About 7:00 a.m. we'll enjoy Lin's cranberry muffins and piping hot coffee. We may canoe upstream to see what we can see. There will be lots of wildlife. And plenty of peace and quiet too. We'll converse with the dog.

And we'll see a lot of ducks. Tonight, we'll roast a couple if we are lucky today. Actually, we are lucky, regardless of whether we bagged our supper. We're in the marsh this morning. Perhaps you heard us.

Still missing my duck hunting buddy

In 1988 my sister Edie was godparent to a litter of Chesapeake Bay Retrievers – seven little bundles of energy in dark coats, two with light saw-grass coverings which seemed ideal for hiding in the swale grass of nearby Hopkins Stream, my duck hunting paradise.

Oh, how I wanted one! And I engaged my kids, ages three and six, in the effort to convince wife Linda that we needed one. We visited the pups more than once. I pleaded. She demurred, more strongly. Finally, that magic moment came when a pup looked into Linda's eyes and she melted. I was ecstatic that it was one of the saw-grass males. I seized the moment and we were home with the pup before Linda had a chance to change her mind.

Dad quickly rehabilitated the old chicken house out back for the puppy's outdoor recreational needs, and we debated names. Blake Hill Buddy was the final choice (we live on Blake Hill Road), Blake for short. And he really was a bundle of joy and energy.

NOTE: I just read the previous sentence to Linda, and she remembers Blake a bit differently! More about that later.

It was Blake's energy that got to be a problem. Determined to train Blake myself, I plunged into the training books, including *Water Dog* by Richard Wolters and *How To Be Your Dog's Best Friend* by the Monks of New Skete. Both are excellent.

Blake was a quick study, actually retrieving dummies and duck wings in the water by the time he was four months old, trained to the whistle and holding steady. Cementing that bond between master and dog which is so important, I kept him by my side throughout the day, as much as possible, his leash wrapped around my ankle. We looked quite a sight stumbling around the house and office.

It was when I took the leash off that trouble began. I gave Blake the run of the house and he quickly sensed that this was his domain, and everything in it. This was the period when he bit some rather large chunks out of our new couch, chewed the coffee table a bit, and ate some of the kids' clothes and toys.

NOTE: Linda says Blake ate a My Child Doll that she had just purchased for Hilary. Linda had made the doll a Christmas nightgown that matched one she'd made for Hilary. Blake ate the face of the doll and tore the nightgown to pieces. "How do you explain that to a three-year-old child?" she asked. Hmmmm.

It also became apparent that I had failed to properly potty train Blake. I trained him on paper. Found out later from the Monks of New Skete that this was a grave mistake! So it was off to the Kennel Shop in Augusta for a large kennel, in which Blake was quickly potty trained and settled into an excellent routine (and yes, this is according to my memory, not Linda's).

Dreaming of ducks

Sitting in my office that June, I watched ducks barreling into Hopkins Pond and Stream, thinking about all the fun ahead. Sure, Blake had cost more money so far than anticipated. I promised

Linda he'd have a light appetite and be a relatively small dog. He ate like a horse and at eight months of age was already huge.

Sure, the furniture he chewed on was new and expensive, and we had to replace some of the kids' toys and clothes. I know. I know. That kennel was expensive. So were the training books, training paraphernalia, collars, leashes, and those five feeding dishes he destroyed before I turned to a metal bucket.

But when he takes that first plunge into Hopkins Stream to retrieve my downed duck the next fall, I knew it would all be worth it. It really would. That's what I told Linda. Many times. And always, she responded, "It would have been easier and cheaper to go to the Village Inn in Belgrade Lakes and order their roast duck." You can't argue with that kind of logic!

Duck hunting

Our first year was a challenge, but when the 1989 season arrived, I felt confident that Blake and I were now a team. As I paddled across "my" beaver bog, the handsome Blake sitting in the front seat of our dinghy, a bunch of black ducks rose to our left out of the weeds, and a cow moose with twins splashed to shore on our right. We passed the huge beaver house as we glided into a small island in the middle of the bog.

A startlingly beautiful red sunrise, which could have graced the walls of any art museum, blessed us as we settled into our island blind. Actually, that entire 12' x 20' island served as our blind, and we wandered about, depending on where the ducks were. They landed all around us.

At first light, the ducks were moving and action was brisk. We quickly downed a black duck, and Blake bounded into the water to retrieve it. In that instant, as he leaped out of the blind and into the water, I couldn't imagine a greater hunting thrill. Although I know it comes naturally to this breed of dog, I also believed my training polished Blake's considerable skills. Oh, if only we could do this every day for the rest of our lives!

Action slowed after the first hour and by 8:00 we were enjoying a hot drink and blueberry muffin as an otter paddled past. We could hear the chop, chop, chop of a beaver in the nearby woods. Blake's ears picked up and a fraction of a second later, goose bumps rose from my forearms. From somewhere over the hill to the east, the haunting honking of a gaggle of geese floated down into our bog. Dropping the drink and muffin, I hunkered down with Blake, praying for a miracle, letting our eyes take only short peaks at the horizon.

Alas, the geese stayed to the east and moved along toward the Maine coast. But we remained thrilled by just the possibility that, as they did once before, the geese would alight all around our tiny island and provide an entree for a memorable meal.

At 8:30 we pick up the decoys, startled a beaver returning to his house, and paddled back across the bog. We'd bagged two ducks, our limit on each species, and enjoyed a finest kind of morning. And we'd be back the next morning!

Later that season

The canoe glided along Hopkins Stream, leaving only the slightest of wakes. I dipped the paddle once to skirt past an exposed boulder and we rounded a bend. Blake was on full alert in the front of the canoe. My Remington 12-gauge 870 magnum pump was on my lap, loaded with 1/38 oz. number 2 shot.

The small body of a hen mallard emerged from the reeds just ahead on our right, as I quickly let off the safety and lifted the shotgun to my shoulder. The stream's current cooperated, tilting the front of the canoe just enough to the left so I was facing the mallard. As the duck lifted off, I had a very easy shot, about 20 yards, straight away. She went down. But I was unprepared for what happened next.

At the sound of my shot, a dozen black ducks erupted from the reeds beside us. Quickly pumping out my first shell, I had another easy opportunity, only about 15 yards, wings spread, looking about the size of an eagle at that range. Hard to miss. And I didn't.

At this point, unable to contain himself any longer, Blake bounded out of the canoe to retrieve the first bird. Barishnikov he isn't, but he managed to jump cleanly over the side of the canoe without dumping me into the stream with him. He quickly brought the first bird to me, still sitting in the canoe mid-stream, and I pointed him back to bird number two, which he also retrieved. Both were dead, part of a string of five successful killing shots I made that morning, a far cry from the previous season when I had real trouble adjusting to the new steel shot requirement.

When Blake tried to get back into the canoe, disaster loomed and I called him off, paddling quickly to shore, where he was able to step in without incident.

A memorable morning, and when it was over, we had our personal limit of ducks and a bag full of new hunting stories. We'd started the day in a quiet beaver bog, and ended it poking around in the flooded alders behind the beaver dam located beside our house.

He's gone

After ten memorable years of hunting with Blake, he started limping, eventually finding it hard to stand. The vet said he was suffering a degenerative hip problem, and, on our final visit there, he told me Blake was much worse and needed to be put down.

It was, as you can imagine, a very tough decision, but I agreed, and went outside to stand by my vehicle while Blake was put to sleep. When the vet came out to tell me it was over, I was standing there bawling like a baby. His assurance that Blake's suffering was over, and that I'd done the right thing, helped a little, but I miss my duck hunting buddy still, 18 years after he died.

I tried hunting without a dog the next fall, a very unsatisfying experience, and I stopped duck hunting altogether for a while. Now I make sure I have friends with dogs, so I can get out a few times. I always reminisce about Blake when I am duck hunting, and will never forget him or the good times we enjoyed.

On the trail of a bear–a novice's experiences hunting bears in Maine

Many years ago, I was sent to bear camp in the Rangeley region to write a story for The Maine Sportsman. *As this year's bear hunting season kicks off, I want to share that story with you. It's a long story, so grab your favorite beverage and settle into a comfortable chair, before you begin! I think you will particularly enjoy the story of Bank Bear so be sure to get to that.*

"It's the most thrilling experience I know."

Those were the words of our guide, David Mangin, owner of Kennebago Guide Service in Rangeley, Maine. I took Dave's comments to be an exaggeration, before our Maine bear hunt began. By the time our hunt ended, I had reached a far different conclusion.

I arrived at the lakeside base camp north of Rangeley on Sunday, August 30, 1987, with an attitude generally shared by many non-bear hunters. I couldn't generate much excitement for the prospect of sitting over bait for hours on end, waiting for a bear to show up so I could shoot it.

Dave's sports arrived throughout the next 24 hours from several states with many different weapons. Sunday afternoon we sighted in our equipment at Dave's gravel pit. The bow hunters shot first. They were from southeast Ohio, with West Virginia accents to prove it. Randy Gilmore of Ironton, Greg Pennington of Hanging Rock, and Glenn Graff of Franklin Furnace had hunted deer in a number of states and black bear in Canada. This was their first trip to Maine.

As I stood off to the side, taking photographs, their arrows whizzed by me at tremendous speed. Those compound bows with 66 pounds of pressure are awesomely powerful.

Next came Paul Hoskins of Walton, Kentucky, with his black powder rifle. Shooting a huge ball, that rifle had all of us with our hands over our ears. What a blast! Nearly everyone fired it at least once, then stood back to wait for their hearing to return! The rest of us carried more conventional weapons. Most had 30.06 rifles, although there was a variety of other guns too, including handguns.

Steve Blood and Scott Lamson of Barre, Vermont, Scott Sahlstorn and Ed Thompson of Nanuet, New York, and Wade Masure and Louie Shattuck of Bellows Falls, Vermont, rounded out the shooting contingent, after Lou Carrier of Winthrop (Mangin's father-in-law), Chip Woodman (Mangin's assistant) and I got in our shooting. Everyone was on target and it was clear that we had some very fine shooters assembled to launch this bear attack on Tuesday, when the 1987 season would open.

Scott Lamson and Paul Hoskins were repeat customers. Scott took home a 200-pound bear the previous year. Paul had terrible luck in 1986. One day he found a bear already lunching at his bait stand when he walked in at 3:00 p.m. The bear took off before Paul could get his black powder rifle loaded. The next day his flintlock misfired on a second bear. Paul was determined to succeed in this, his third attempt at a Maine bear. Although he had to set aside his black powder rifle for something more conventional to change his luck, he would finally go home with a Maine bear.

Monday dawned fair and cool, as we struck out to bait our stands and get acquainted with our hunting territory. Dave had set up almost three dozen stands originally, but was now concentrating on about 15 of them.

Accompanying Dave on his baiting rounds, I began to get a feel for the exciting experience bear hunting can be. Seeing the onion skin bait bags ripped to shreds, some ten feet or more off the ground, examining the massive tracks of some of the bruins now traveling in that area, and studying the tree stands which in many cases are no more than 15 yards from the bait, my eyes were opened to the very real possibility of a supremely close encounter with a large black bear.

All of Dave's baits had been hit throughout the summer and he reported that prospects for a successful hunt were high. As we traveled from bait to bait that Monday morning, replenishing the many baits that bears had hit the previous night, my enthusiasm rose ever higher. For the first time, I began to think I might actually shoot a bear.

The stands ranged from 100 to 300 yards off the many dirt roads surrounding Rangeley, some in low boggy areas, others on ridges. Each spot was arranged with a large tree stand and seat facing the bait bag attached to a nearby tree. My assigned stand looked very promising, on a high ridge with an active trail passing right behind my bait tree. Very large bear tracks could be seen there in the mud and I began to sweat for the first time, contemplating the size of some of the bruins that had by now made my stand a regular stop on their eating binges. I told Dave I was sweating and breathing hard because of the walk up the hill to the stand. However, I knew there was something more, as well.

We spent much of the rest of Monday getting our gear in order and getting acquainted with each other. I found varying degrees of dedication. Scott Sahlstron put his camouflage hunting clothes right next to the bait bucket! Boy, did they stink! The rest of us settled for garbage bags filled with fragrant spruce limbs, after airing the clothes out on a line for much of the day.

Bears do not see well, I learned, but they have an extraordinary sense of smell. That being the case, I expected one bear would find Scott very delectable indeed! Dave provided us all with cover scents which I noticed lingered for many days afterward on my clothes. The scents were very effective.

For the final year, this year's hunt was scheduled to begin on September first. In 1988, it will start on the Monday of the first partial week in September, meaning the opening might actually be in late August of a transition week from August to September. Unfortunately, this year we had to wait all day Monday for Tuesday's opening bell. That just built up our anticipation.

It starts!

Tuesday dawned cold and clear, but with a steady wind which made our guide all the more nervous. I was starting to get a sense of the pressure which a professional Maine guide can feel as he seeks to put together a successful hunt for his sports. Mangin takes his job very seriously and strives, successfully in my opinion, to put on an exciting hunt. Dave's sneakers wore a path back and forth in the rug of our base camp as Tuesday progressed.

We were out baiting again after a tremendous breakfast of bacon, eggs, home fries, beans, toast, muffins, orange juice, coffee, and pie for dessert. Incredibly, we ate like this every single meal. I gained four pounds during the week!

Monday night's dinner had included bear meat and I was now convinced that the sports who had told me it was inedible just hadn't known how to prepare it. We all found it positively delicious and were now more than ever anxious to fill our home freezers with those delectable bear steaks.

Our guide wasn't the only nervous one as the week began. Steve Blood of Vermont was up all of Monday night, spending much of it riding around the countryside, counting moose and deer. I heard him pull into camp about 5:30 a.m. Tuesday morning, much the worse for wear.

Throughout the week we enjoyed glimpses of every wild critter this country holds, including grouse, coons, foxes, hawks and owls, lots of moose, and more deer than I have ever seen in this neck of the woods, a very good sign that our bucks-only seasons are working here.

But of course we were here to see bear and it was finally time to head to our stands. We got into our camo clothing, broke into small groups, and jumped into the vehicles. I rode out to the ridge with Scott Lamson and Steve Blood, who were on stands to each side of me, each about two miles distant.

The bowhunters were isolated in their own area and the remaining rifle hunters were dispersed over an area of about 15 square miles. For the first time, we encountered other hunters, some of whom had located new stands terribly close to Mangin's stands. Lack of sportsmanship began to rear its ugly head, as these other hunters tried to take advantage of our baits. It was troubling, to say the least.

On this first night, Wade Masure was most severely impacted, as one member of a gang of hunters shot at a bear about 150 feet from Wade's stand. He apparently missed but Wade's stand was ruined. He moved to another the next night, and found a bow hunter stationed just 30 feet behind him at his new stand!

Dave had us all on stands by 2:30 p.m. and I had already begun to find my seat rather uncomfortable by 4:00 p.m. Hunting deer from stands has always been a favorite tactic of mine, but I am rarely able to sit still for more than an hour and a half. Now I was called on to sit still for over five hours! Worse, I could not read, eat, or take it easy for even a minute. My stand was in thick growth and Dave had told me a bear might slip into the area without the slightest sound, so I had to be alert at all times.

Have you ever tried to concentrate on a single thing for five hours, to sit still, not day dream, and pay the closest attention to every detail around you? Well, I was some surprised to find out how exciting this could be! The red squirrels and grouse, louder than any bear could possibly be, nevertheless led me to believe that a bear was approaching about every 15 minutes. I also learned that you do not fall out of a tree stand even if your fanny falls asleep!

The essence of bear hunting was conveyed to me on that first very windy night when no self-respecting bear was out and about. Anticipation. Suspense. Nerves as the darkness descends and you spend that last half hour of legal shooting time after sunset on tinder hooks, imagining that every dark rock in the surrounding forest is an approaching bear, bent on eating your bait and then having you for dessert!

As I emptied my gun, bearless on Tuesday evening, climbed down from my stand, turned to the path out with my trusty flashlight pointing the way, wind still howling in the trees, a terrible shiver still pulsing through my body since I had discovered an hour earlier that I had not dressed warmly enough, I could not have been more enthusiastic. Bear hunting had taken a firm grip on me and I was not to be denied. I loved it!

What was it that had turned me around on this sport? I gave that question a lot of thought as I sat on that stand for the next few days. Perhaps it was finding out that bear hunting is far from a sure thing. It is in fact tough hunting, requiring incredible patience, fortitude, and will. A certain degree of skill is also involved, although the guide fills in many areas in this regard, from providing proper bait and cover scents to putting you in the right place. But the guide also allows you to do as much on your own as you desire.

Perhaps my enthusiasm developed as I saw those claw marks above some of the baits on that first day, or walked in to the stands in such incredibly beautiful surroundings. I'd never hunted anything in September before and this new experience was so pleasant that I wouldn't have cared if we were hunting bear or water buffalo. It was great to be out in the woods hunting.

Most of all, after talking with Dave Mangin and those sports who had hunted black bear before, I guess I developed a tremendous respect for the animal we sought that week. Sure, he has a sharp hunger which brings him in to our baits. But he comes in warily, guided by a supersensitive nose, aware of the slightest odor out of place. This heavy beast walks in slippers on the quietest of forest floors. Hundreds of pounds, he moves with the grace of a ballet dancer and the quickness of a flyweight boxer. Terribly difficult to bring down, as we would find out first hand on Wednesday evening, the Maine black bear is a game animal of the first order. I was excited to be hunting him!

Although the wind caused us all problems on Tuesday's hunt, Louis Shattuck did have a small bear wander in to his stand at 5:45 p.m. that night. The bear entered the area without a sound and Louie looked up to find the bear nearly at his bait. The approximately 100-pound bruin stayed for more than an hour. He sniffed the bait. Leaped into the bushes. Came back. Walked around, sniffing loudly. He didn't eat, but simply wandered off the way he'd come. "Too small," Louis told us. "Maybe tomorrow night he'll be bigger!"

Glenn Graff also saw a bear about 3:30 p.m. about 100 yards above him on the ridge but it never approached his bait. Dave was all the more nervous after a night with no bear on the game pole. But Wednesday promised better conditions, perhaps.

Wednesday – action!

I had to return home for my boy's first day of kindergarten and a Selectman's meeting on Wednesday night, so I missed our first real action of the week's hunt.

Although it was again very windy on Wednesday, at 5:10 p.m. Greg Pennington had a bear come in to his bait. It just ambled straight in, a nice sized bear. Before he got to the bait, he quartered to Greg and Greg got off an arrow. The arrow went right through the bear, somewhere behind the front shoulders, probably a bit low. The wounded bear took off.

Greg got down and retrieved his arrow and had been back in his stand for about ten minutes when a second bear, about the same size, came in to his bait. Not knowing the condition of the first bear he'd shot at, Greg did not fire at the second. A fruitless search the next morning found a slight blood trail for about a half mile, then nothing. Most agreed that the bear would live to fight another day. Greg, however, felt terrible. He would not see another bear that week.

Also on Wednesday night, a bear came in behind Scott Sahlstorn about 7 p.m. He heard him coming but it took a half hour for the bear to arrive at the bait site. At 7:30 p.m. the bear's growl told Scott that he was close, but not close enough. Flipping over rocks, the bear came within 50 yards, finally stopping behind a pine tree. Scott neither saw nor heard him again. Checking the area on his way out, Scott could find nothing. But the next morning his bait had been cleaned out. Apparently that bear retreated a short ways until Scott left, then came in for his feed.

As Scott Lamson was approaching camp on his way in from hunting on Wednesday, he and Steve Blood encountered a 200 plus pound bear bounding across the road in front of them. A second smaller bear would also be seen on the final morning by Chip Woodman in this same area, no more than a half mile from camp, as Chip motored by on an ATV, without his gun!

Lou Carrier had a large cow moose walk right up to his stand on Wednesday night, practically looking him in the eye. It was the first of many sightings of moose, deer, and other wildlife from our stands.

Thursday – I return

I returned Thursday noon in time to join in another big meal and hear about the fabulous moose chop suey that had been on the menu for Wednesday night's dinner. I also received word that my bait had been hit after I left it Tuesday night, the second night in a row that a bruin had visited my stand. Unfortunately, it would be the last time that week that my bait was hit.

Tension was building now and our guide had spent a sleepless night worrying about the weather. Wednesday the wind had also blown a gale, leaving us bearless but not surly. The sports were taking it well. No one had lost confidence. Everyone was well fed, fat, and happy! Our guide, however, was close to being a wreck. Two nights of hunting and no bears yet!

The wind was slightly diminished Thursday but still blowing. Conditions were far from ideal although it was cool. We had all added long underwear and heavier clothing after getting chilled on Tuesday night so we were at least comfortable tonight.

At 6:00 p.m. Louie had his second sighting, a bear that came in head-on, the wind blowing in his face. Before the bear got to the bait, Louie shot it just behind the front shoulders (Dave had instructed us to go for a shoulder shot first, which prevents the bear from running off, and allows for a quick and easy finishing shot). Louie's bear took off to his left and he very professionally

81

put a second bullet into its spine. It dropped immediately and Louie began the task of getting his nerves under control. It was only the second bear he had ever seen, the first coming the evening before, and he was shaking like a wind-blown autumn leaf! Shooting a bear was an incredible experience!

Mark Ryan of Rangeley, Dave's sometime hunting and guiding partner and houndsman, had one of his sports from Maryland shoot a bear on this night too, after taking some photos of the bruin walking around the stand! No other sightings on Thursday but Louie has broken the ice and the rest of us couldn't do enough for him as Friday dawned.

Now I must add a word here about camp life. Evening poker was the order of the day, and although our guide did well the first night, Glenn Graff had cleaned everyone out by Friday. A ringer from Ohio! We all slept cheek to jowl in an attached bunkhouse and some of the guys talked in their sleep. Randy Gilmore of Ohio discussed bow hunting at some length while asleep one night and Scott Sahlstron literally shouted out some rather interesting things another night. I recorded Scott's remarks, as any good reporter would, but can't convey them to you. Perhaps *Penthouse* magazine would be interested?!

Camp life settled into a very nice routine, big breakfast, get the stands baited, swim or go to town to see the sights, big lunch, nap, get ready to hunt, hunt, big dinner, good conversations, beer and cards before bed. Bear hunting is certainly a leisurely pursuit. And by Friday, the only thing most of us lacked was a bear.

Lucky Friday

On Friday we would finally get a break in the weather. It was a very hot day, in the 80s, with a slight breeze. Calm winds were expected for the prime hunting hours of 5:00 p.m. to 7:30 p.m. We were all confident that bears would be shot tonight. Someone had to connect before our guide self-destructed from worry! Tonight, his spirits would be lifted.

On Friday morning we all took photographs of Louie and his bear, then drove to Cupsuptic Campground to weigh the bruin. Getting lots of stares and comments from campers there, Louie's bear weighed a very respectable 150 pounds. That's about average for a Maine black bear. Anything over 200 pounds is big. We would find out how big the next night. We kept the campground stirred up as we brought in our bears on Friday and Saturday mornings.

From the campground it was on to Oquossoc to tag Louie's bear, then over to Mark Ryan's house to get it on the game pole. More photos. Mark skinned the bear out while we were there, and later carved out a good pile of steaks for Louie to take home in his cooler. The head and coat were frozen for delivery to a nearby taxidermist. Louie ordered a bear rug, certain to be a topic of conversation at his house in Vermont.

The winds had died almost completely when we returned to camp, and we eagerly ate lunch and got ready for the hunt. By now some of us weren't going out on stand until 4 pm, finding that 4 hours in the stand was our physical limit. I of course was one of the laggards.

But we knew Friday was going to be a really good chance, with no wind to keep the bears wary and away, so we all got out on stand by mid-afternoon. It really started for us at 5 pm when Scott Sahlstorn shot at a coyote that had wandered into his area. Scott missed and assumed that would end his chances for a bear that night. But he was wrong. Two hours later he heard a bear approach and carefully let off the safety on his 30.06 when the bear poked his head up over a stump.

As the 140-pound sow moved through a small opening to Scott's left, it smelled Scott and took off at a gallop. Guess the bear didn't care for those clothes soaked in bear bait, after all! Scott quickly fired four shots and the bear dropped in her tracks.

An hour earlier, a 140-pound boar came in to Glenn Graff's bait and Glenn embedded a broadhead in the bait tree. The bear took off. But one of the many advantages of bow hunting that I learned this week is that a missed shot does not a missed opportunity make. Unsure of what happened, that bear came right back to Glenn's bait five minutes later and this time he made a sure shot, the arrow traveling completely through the bear, a lung and shoulder shot.

As Dave had instructed, Glenn stayed in his stand until closing time, then walked out and returned to camp to notify us of his bear. That notification would cause quite a commotion because Glenn pulled into camp right behind Scott Lamson, Steve Blood, and I, returning to report that Scott had also shot a bear!

Herm Giles of Monmouth had just arrived at camp, one of several sports who would stop by for a day or two during the week, and he had dinner underway including some fine moose meat from Herm's 1986 moose. It looked mighty tempting but it was put on hold as we took off in different directions to try to bring in the bears that Glenn and Scott had shot.

It happened to be Glenn's anniversary and he had to send Randy out to Oquossoc to phone his wife and let her know that his anniversary call would be late tonight. He had a bear to find! I did not learn how that message was received by Mrs. Graff.

Dave also had Randy call Mark Ryan in Rangeley and ask him to meet them at Glenn's stand with Mark's hounds. Dave, Glenn, Herm and Greg headed out to meet Mark at the stand. The hounds took only a few minutes to find that bear where he had dropped about 100 yards from the stand. Glenn's shot had been a good one. Paul Hoskins came with Mark and was heartily congratulated on shooting his own sow that evening. Things were hopping!

Meanwhile, I had been dropped off to help Scott Lamson haul his bruin up out of a bog. Steve Blood, Wade Masure, and Louis Shattuck joined us for a memorable experience.

The Bank Bear

This is the story of the "Bank Bear." As you read this, the Bank Bear is in Vermont, preparing to be a magnificent, if somewhat scarred, rug. He is partially eaten already, by the Lamson family, which professes to love bear meat. Having now had that meat, I can't disagree. Our guide claimed on Day One that bear meat is his favorite, and by the week's end he had won many converts, including yours truly.

But prior to this night, the Bank Bear had lived in the bogs and along the ridges of the Rangeley country. Dave Mangin first made his acquaintance in the summer of 1986, when he noticed a deep ravine below a dirt road in the back country where he has so many of his bait stands. Setting a bait about 100 yards into the steep ravine along the bank, Dave found it gone the next day. Without putting up a tree stand, Dave kept baiting that area. The Bank Bear obligingly kept eating.

In the fall Dave moved the bait another 100 yards toward the bog below and in the summer of 1987 he built a tree stand about 25 yards from the bait, now positioned 200 yards off the road at the bottom of the ravine just outside the bog which lay between this site and a high mountain. Dave figured that the bear spent his days in the coolness of the bog. And from the huge paw prints, he knew that this bear was something special, far above 200 pounds

And he was right. Scott Lamson had come to Maine the year before and taken home a very nice 200-pound bear, but he had also helped Dave set baits out for the Bank Bear and he desperately wanted a crack at him this year. Scott even came back to Maine earlier in the summer of 1987 to help Dave bait and to take another look at the habitat of the Bank Bear. He was obsessed by now with the size and cunning of this bruin.

Dave allowed as how Scott could give it a try this fall, if he wanted to, and Scott quickly confirmed his reservation for a hunt during the first week of the season. He wanted first crack at Bank Bear! Scott dutifully baited his stand on Sunday, Monday, Tuesday, Wednesday, and Thursday. It was never hit. As the week progressed, he began to get discouraged. But he didn't give up. It was going to be the Bank Bear or nothing for him this year.

When he walked in to his stand on Friday afternoon, the next to last chance he would have at the Bank Bear, the hair on the back of Scott's neck stood right up. His bait had been hit. The Bank Bear had struck again! Best of all the Bank Bear had eaten two bags of bait but left a third bag untouched. "That bear knows there is one more bag of bait and he'll be back for it," Scott thought. "This is going to be my night!"

At 7:30 p.m., as darkness settled in and shooting time waned, Scott saw a bear off to his right in some heavy brush. He couldn't tell the size, and when it dropped down toward the bog he assumed he'd lost his opportunity. It must have picked up his scent and wandered off into the bog. Scott could have taken a shot into the brush, but felt it was not a very good shot and he passed. Less than a minute later, Bank Bear reared up on his hind legs about forty feet in front of Scott, down in the bog. He had dropped down into the bog, but now he was coming back!

As he came up over a downed tree and reared up, Scott calmly put two bullets into him, in the neck and shoulder. Bank Bear dropped to the ground. Heart pounding, sweat streaming down his face even on this cool evening, Scott began to descend carefully from his stand. Halfway down, he glanced over and there was Bank Bear, growling and standing in place with his two huge front paws waving at Scott. Bank Bear was furious!

Now, you or I would have climbed right back up into the tree stand, and that's probably what our guide would have recommended. But Scott had only a second to reach a decision and he went for it. Dropping all the way to the ground, Scott landed with a thud, quickly squared around toward Bank Bear, and pumped two more shots in his direction. We would speculate the next day as to whether he hit the bear again. Those shots were not readily apparent on the bear's hide.

But no matter, Bank Bear dropped down again, this time for good. Catching his breath, Scott scampered back up into his stand and tried to collect himself. It was nearly pitch dark now but he could see Bank Bear below him, not moving. As Scott's heart rate eased up a bit and his cool night's breath came in quieter gasps, elation seized him. After two years of careful baiting, the Bank Bear had been felled. And he was huge.

As Scott and Steve and Wade and Louie and I dragged Bank Bear those 200 yards straight up hill to the road, we speculated wildly about his weight. He was certainly the biggest bear I'd ever seen in Maine. Just as round as Old St. Nick, with paws that dwarfed my hands, and stretching nearly six feet along the ground, there was no disputing that Bank Bear was a trophy animal.

The next day at Cupsuptic Campground he would weigh in at a firm 300 pounds, dressed weight. From head to toe Bank Bear was covered with scars, including a new open wound on his face. We all speculated that we'd like to see the other bear that wounded Bank Bear.

We didn't know it on Saturday morning as we loaded up Mark Ryan's game pole with the three bears we'd gotten the night before to go with the bear Mark had guided Paul Hoskins to, but we had reached our peak on Friday night. Paul had finally changed his luck by leaving his black powder rifle home and taking a 150-pound sow with a more conventional rifle. After three years of hunting Maine black bear, Paul was delighted and we were happy for him.

Those four bears hanging on the game pole were quite a sight. And the rest of us were now more determined than ever to add our own bears to the pole on Saturday night. Alas, we must wait until next year.

Final day

Saturday was hot and sticky leading many of us into the lake for a swim. We got out on the stands early, though, anticipating another night like Friday night and not wanting to miss a minute of it.

The day had gotten off to a fast start as a houndsman had struck his dogs above our camp at about 5:30 am and they had howled right on down our camp road to the three bruins we had laying on the front lawn. That houndsman was some old embarrassed as he gathered those hounds up.

Saturday afternoon waged on, very hot with no wind. The bears apparently found it too hot to move. No one saw a bear this day. Steve enjoyed a sleek doe and two skippers which wandered into his stand and stayed around for a half hour, and I took note that this would be a good hardwood stand during deer season. But the bears were taking it easy and we added no bruins to the game pole.

As some sports packed up for a long and late Saturday night ride home, others began preparations to return home on Sunday morning, and two new hunters arrived from Massachusetts to begin their own week of bear hunting. They would hunt over bait, as we had, while others due to arrive the next day would be hunting with Mark Ryan and his hounds.

Oh, how I longed to tell them what the previous week had meant to me. How could I describe it in all its glorious details? Scott shooting at a coyote and bagging his bear two hours later. Glenn taking down his bear with bow and arrow after Greg lost his. Louis passing on a small bear and shooting a bigger one the next night. Paul getting his bear after three years. And Bank Bear, already growing into a legend that we will all talk about for years to come. Of the eleven paying customers guided by Dave and Mark that first week, six went home with bears. Interestingly, each group from a particular state went home with one bear.

Myself, I had sat for 18 hours on stand, seen an owl attack a grouse, stared at that bait for hours on end, imagined every boulder was a huge bruin as nightfall descended, sat in the final quiet half hour of darkness after sundown listening to the woods, walking out by flashlight on Saturday evening with a song in my head. From reluctant and skeptical hunter on Sunday, I had become a dedicated pursuer of the Maine black bear by the following Saturday.

If time had permitted, I'd have signed up for the next week of hunting right then and there. Steve Blood even called his wife to beg for more money so he could stay another week (he didn't get it). One of the Ohio bow hunters said it was the finest hunt he'd ever experienced. It was not the deer hunt that is my passion, but it was a good and exciting hunt. It was the excitement that surprised me.

The tension in camp, the sleepless nights and nervous days, the incredible anticipation as we waited for a bear to come to the bait, the tremendous amount of work put in by our guide to make it possible for us to be in the right place at the right time with a chance to shoot a bear, all added up to a truly exceptional hunting experience.

Is it the most thrilling thing you can do? Well, I don't know. Each hunter has to make up his own mind about that. It is certainly that to Dave Mangin who has the skills to find bears and bring them in to his hunters. Yet Dave doesn't sit in a stand and hunt bears himself. He won't compete with his hunters. Dave prefers the satisfaction of sending those hunters home with this trophy Maine game animal, knowing that the guide was a critical factor in the hunt and that he, Dave Mangin, had given that sport a very special hunting experience. And it is certainly that to Scott Lamson who joined Dave in stalking Bank Bear for two years before bringing him down. For the rest of us, yes, it was a thrilling hunt. Most immediately made plans to return in 1988.

Footnote: Today, the seasons of hunting over bait and with hounds are separated. Shortly after my 1987 hunt, my wife Linda saw Dave Mangin, who said, "Boy, your husband can really eat!" It's nice to have a reputation for being good at something.

Turkey hunting is challenging and fun

I blame Harry Vanderweide. He got me into turkey hunting and it became an obsession, both in the field and in the legislature. I've had quite a bit of success in both places. In 2014, the legislature enacted a bunch of changes that Senator Tom Saviello submitted in a bill at my request.

The bill reduced the turkey hunting permit to $20 for both residents and nonresidents, with no additional fee for a second Tom in the spring, authorized all-day hunting for youth day, expanded the fall season to the entire month of October and added a second turkey of either sex to the fall bag limit, reduced the

89

tagging fee from $5 to $2, and extended the spring hunt to all day (one half hour before sunrise to one half hour after sunset).

What was I thinking? All day turkey hunting? Yikes! Now I can't get anything done during the turkey season. Well, turkey hunting is lots of fun, especially the spring hunt where you can call in the gobblers with a hen call. In the fall, you have to intercept them or run them down. And yes, I've done that. Here are stories about some of my favorite turkey hunts.

My first turkey

I shot my first turkey in the fields above my house in Mount Vernon. Harry and I came down the wooded hillside before dawn to see a gobbler and two hens in the field along with six deer. It was dark enough that Harry could creep out into the field and put up one decoy. And then we were astonished to see the gobbler jump on one of the hens and have his way with her. Amazingly, the deer came over and stood around watching them! Voyeurs! While the gobbler was having his fun with one of the hens, the other hen wandered off into the woods.

When the gobbler hopped off the hen, he started in the direction of the other hen, and I whispered to Harry, "Can I shoot now?" I was sure I could hit the gobbler – he was only about 150 yards away. Well, if you are a turkey hunter, you know that that is a ridiculously long distance to try to shoot a turkey. I didn't know that at the time.

As the gobbler approached the woods, about 100 yards off to our left, I asked again, "Can I shoot now? It's getting away!" Harry said to hold my fire. And he started calling. Much to my surprise, the gobbler turned sharply in our direction and started our way.

Twice, before he got there, I asked if I could shoot, and got a firm no. I didn't ask the last time when I shot the gobbler about 10 yards in front of us! Harry said, "That's the easiest turkey hunt you will ever experience." And he was right!

Dad's first hunt

After my first year of turkey hunting with Harry, when we had great luck hunting west of Augusta, especially in Windsor and Somerville, I tried to interest Dad in joining us, but he didn't want to pay the $8 fee, so I paid it for him. I never had to do that again! He loved turkey hunting.

That first year with Dad, we had permission to hunt a strawberry field in Windsor, and as we drove along the field, we spotted turkeys up ahead, right near the road. Dad was ready to jump out and get after them, but Harry explained he'd never be able to get close to them. But Dad insisted, so Harry stopped and he hopped out.

Somehow, he managed to keep the only big tree alongside the road between him and the turkeys, and when he got to the tree, he peaked around it, raised his gun, and shot. By golly he got a nice big Tom! And he was some tickled. I've got another story from this spot to share with you at the end of this column.

One memorable hunt occurred out back of Harry's daughter Amanda's house in West Gardiner. We were in a tent, and Harry fired an arrow that passed right through a turkey. But it ran off and we never found it. Yes, turkeys are tough!

Coyotes joined us

Ever since this happened, I've assumed that coyotes kill and eat a lot of turkeys. Harry, Dad, and I were in our turkey blind in Windsor, in the woods and surrounded by brush, sitting in the dark waiting for dawn, when a coyote jumped out of the bushes and came down right on top of one of our turkey decoys.

He quickly figured out that the decoy was not going to be very tasty and bounded off before any of us could get off a shot at him. The next morning when we returned to the same place, Dad brought a bunch of traps and set them up all around the decoys! But we never saw that coyote again.

91

One year, I was turkey hunting alone in Mount Vernon, hidden behind a rock wall with my decoys in a field in front of me, when I saw a coyote with a beautiful golden coat emerge from the woods about 200 yards away and start trotting my way. He came right up to my decoys, decided they weren't what he was hoping for, and turned around, never breaking stride, trotting back across the field and into the woods. I made the mistake of writing about this in my *Outdoor News* blog and got roasted by some readers for not shooting the coyote.

Bobcats love turkeys too. One winter morning, I noticed a bunch of turkey feathers in the snow under an apple tree in our back yard. It wasn't difficult to figure out what happened, from the tracks in the snow. A bobcat had sat in the crotch of the tree and jumped on a turkey when it passed beneath him. The remains of the turkey were in the bushes about 10 yards away.

Chasing one down

Eventually we spent less time hunting east of Augusta and more hunting around Mount Vernon and Fayette, where we had great luck, including on my woodlot.

One time Harry and I were at Steep Hill Farm in Fayette, sitting in a grove of oak trees on the back side of their woodlot, within sight of a huge hillside that had been heavily cut by the neighboring landowner. We'd just put out the decoys and started calling when a gobbler answered Harry. The gobbler was out in the clearcut, so we walked down to the edge of the woodlot we were in and Harry called again. The gobbler answered again, but he seemed farther away.

We decided he must be with a group of hens and walking away from us, so Harry stayed put, calling continuously, while I took off after the turkeys. I hiked through the first clearing, then had to wait while they moved through the next one (so they wouldn't see me). The gobbler was still answering Harry's calls, so I walked through the second clearing after the turkeys had cleared it.

When I got to the far edge of that cut, the woods ahead were thicker, so I kept moving, eventually getting to a woods road. A sharp hill rose on the far side of the road, and the gobbler was up there, calling back to Harry. So I crawled up the hill, and as I approached the top, I could peek out between a stonewall and a huge downed tree. And there he was! Sitting on a stump just 20 feet away, facing me, calling to Harry. I raised my shotgun and shot through the small opening, and down he went. On my scale at home, he weighed 23.5 pounds, a real beauty.

Kennebec River

Harry, his adult daughter Amanda (who had only recently taken up hunting) and I boated down the Kennebec River, stopping here and there so Harry could use his hen call. When we got a bunch of excited gobbles in response, we boated to shore, climbed a hill, and sat. Amanda was about 30 yards to my left, and Harry was behind me, doing the calling.

The gobblers were roosting in trees a hundred yards or so above us, and we couldn't see them, but they answered Harry's calls for the better part of a half hour, until I decided to set my gun down and enjoy a cup of coffee. I had just poured the cup when I looked up and – wouldn't you know it – here came the turkeys toward us, a huge gobbler in front followed by a string of other gobblers and hens. I froze, not wanting them to spot me.

When they got to within about 30 yards, I quickly picked up my shotgun and they turned and ran. The big gobbler disappeared immediately, running toward Amanda. Another Tom took to the air, so I took aim at him and knocked him down. Amanda shot right after me, so I quickly ran to my Tom, lying dead on the ground, then ran to Amanda. She'd made a good shot and her gobbler was dead, a nice jake. After congratulating her, I walked back to my turkey and – Holy Cow! – he was gone. And we were unable to find him, despite a lengthy search.

Lesson learned

In the last year I hunted turkeys with my Dad, he wasn't able to walk far, so he sat in a chair we'd put up along a stone wall at Steep Hill Farm in Fayette, and I circled around, hoping to chase some turkeys his way. As I approached an opening in the woods, only a few hundred yards from Dad, I spotted a whole bunch of turkeys, and as I approached, they headed down toward Dad. So I followed them for about 50 yards, when they picked up speed, still headed toward Dad. But one nice Tom lingered behind the others, so I shot him, and he dropped.

I walked up to him, figured he was dead, and took off after the other turkeys. But I got only about 20 yards when that hunt with Amanda popped into my head, so I walked back to my dead turkey and – Surprise! – he jumped up and started running. That time, I shot him dead.

The group of turkeys passed to the left of Dad, out of range, but he did see all of them cross the woods roads behind him. That photo of Dad and me with that gobbler is the one I've got up on my Facebook page. I didn't know it at the time, but it was to be the last turkey we got together. By the next turkey season, Dad was in the Hospice unit at Togus, where he died on the last day of October 2014.

Dad's last hunt

Dad was in the Hospice Unit at the Veteran's Hospital at Togus for six months. He wasn't able to hunt in the spring but when the October turkey season opened, he spotted some turkeys on the lawn at Togus, and inquired as to whether he might hunt them, but guns are prohibited on the property, so I got another idea.

I wheeled Dad out to my Subaru one October morning, loaded him into the front passenger seat, and we drove around Windsor and Somerville to all the places we'd hunted turkeys with Harry. It was a wonderful morning, full of great memories.

Astonishingly, as we approached the strawberry farm where Dad shot his first turkey, we spotted a bunch of turkeys. I stopped the vehicle and we watched the birds walk down through the field. Dad urged me to get out and see if I could get close. I did not have my shotgun, but I did get out, to please Dad, and crept down through the woods adjacent to the field, getting close enough to the birds to shoot one if I'd had a gun and wanted to do so.

Dad got quite a kick out of it. And we counted it as our 54th year of hunting together. Three weeks later, Dad died, the night before the opening day of the firearms season on deer. I've often said, I think he died that night because he was so aggravated he couldn't hunt the next day. I wear a piece of Dad's clothing every day now when I'm hunting, so he's still there, with me.

Appreciating one neighbor's generosity

I have spent my career trying to improve relations between sportsmen and landowners, with limited success. In 2015 the legislature enacted a bill I proposed that reorganized the Landowner Sportsmen Relations Advisory Board and created a new program called Keep Maine Clean, *to recruit and organize folks who walk the woods and roads and pick up trash. It's critically important these days that all of us who enjoy recreating on private land ask permission, keep landowners informed of our activities on their properties, and thank them after we're done. This column was my own thank you to my wonderful neighbor Clayton Somers, published in 2006.*

Clayton Somers died on July 23. He meant a lot to me although he probably didn't realize it. A neighbor who lived at the other end of Blake Hill Road, Clayt allowed me to hunt on the 500 acres of land he owned with his wife Barbara. Through the years I got to know their property well.

In the field next to their home, I shot my first 200-pound buck. It was a memorable morning, my best deer hunting day up to that point. Seated on high ground on a stone wall, I saw eight deer run across a lower field and cross Blake Hill Road as the first rays of sunshine touched the pines behind me.

About 7:00 a.m. I relocated near the road where Dad was to pick me up for a hunters' breakfast. Out of the woods behind Clayt's house skipped a doe, and when I put my scope on her, a huge rack of antlers appeared just behind her. The biggest buck I'd ever seen was right on her tail. I actually had to move to get the proper angle to shoot the buck, which I did, careful to avoid shooting directly at Clayt's house.

Four years ago, I shot my first turkey in Clayt's high field. Harry Vanderweide and I set up in Clayt's woods early that morning, watching six deer and three turkeys in the field. Eventually Harry called in a 19-pound Tom and I shot him at about 10 yards. It was incredibly exciting. Without a doubt, one of my best days of turkey hunting.

Over the years, I think Dad and I probably took eight or ten deer off Clayt's land, and enjoyed many fine days of hunting there. His generosity of sharing his land allowed me to build a bank of wonderful memories. Clayt loved deer heart and liver, and I always gave him mine, with a few packages of venison.

It was doubly generous of Clayt to allow this, because he was an avid hunter too. Hunting season found him at his camp on Hopkins Stream that flows past my house. The camp was once a cranberry operation when the stream sported a commercial cranberry business. It's the only camp on the stream and I know Clayt loved it. Occasionally I'd stop at the camp during hunting season to visit, as I canoed downstream to some of my favorite hunting spots.

Clayt's father, Winnie, was one of my favorite people. I first met Winnie on a ridge in the woods above Clayt's fields, where he regaled me for about two hours with hunting tales. I was fascinated by the stories of Winnie's fox hunts across the hills and through the valleys of northern Maine.

But his best hunting stories involved deer hunting in Washington County. He and his hunting buddies would ride the train, get out in the middle of the wild lands that predominated in the county at the time, set up a tent, and hunt until they had taken their limit of deer. Well, actually Winnie shot all of the deer. When Winnie had a deer for each of them, they'd put up a flag and the train would stop and pick them up, the deer piled high in a box car. From that first afternoon on the ridge, I realized that Clayt was a chip off the old block, an outdoorsman in the oldest and finest sense of the word.

I always enjoyed visiting and talking with Clayt. Now, of course, I wish I'd done more of that, especially lately as he grew increasingly housebound. The last time I dropped off venison and had a short visit, he was saddened by his inability to hunt anymore. I shared some of my hunting stories from the past season, a sad turnabout in our relationship.

I wish I'd visited Clayt more often these past couple of years, and now the regret is great. His willingness to share his land made a huge difference in my life. I hope he knew how grateful I am.

Game mistakes (and other weird things)

Oh, the mistakes I've made!

When I started to build a list of all the mistakes I've made while hunting, well, it turns out I made a lot more mistakes than I remembered! I guess that's the trail we take to become successful hunters. For me, the trail was long and sometimes frustrating.

I started off on the wrong foot, when, at the age of nine, I snuck up to a robin, perched on a tree in our front yard, and shot it with my BB gun. Dad explained, quickly, how wrong that was! Seems appropriate that today I am an avid birder. With binoculars, not a shotgun!

About a half century later, I was hunting woodcock with my friend Jimmy Robbins in Searsmont, when we moved into a grown-over apple orchard. Jimmy told me to stand near an old apple tree on a knoll, while he took the dog and hunted down through the thick brush off to our right. He pointed to the far end of that piece and said to watch that spot, because that's where the woodcock would fly out.

Focused intently on that spot, I listened as Jim and the dog moved down through the brush. And there it was! The bird exploded out of the brush right where Jimmy said it would, and I quickly raised my shotgun and made one of the best shots of my life, knocking the bird down as it sped across the clearing in front of me. It went down into the bushes below me.

Jim and the dog emerged right after I shot and I pointed out where the bird had gone down. I knew something was wrong when the dog went over to that spot, looked down, then lifted its head and moved away. Jim went over and picked up the bird. I had shot a robin!

The first time I ever hunted woodcock with Jimmy, we were in a set of alders when the dog pointed a woodcock. I walked over to the bird and it took off. I shot it at about 15 feet. When we walked up to the bird, there was very little left of it. Jimmy kindly explained that, in the future, I should let the bird get out a bit farther before shooting. And he left the bird there, not counting it against my limit for the day.

One snowy day, I exited the house and walked over to Route 41 to hunt the woods there, and almost immediately, I discovered a fresh deer tack. It was good sized, so I took off after it, following it here and there for two hours, down to the stream and back to the road, where it crossed Route 41 about 100 yards east of where I'd started in that morning.

The deer swam across the outlet of Minnehonk Lake, coming ashore in my woodlot right behind my house, then walked through my woods and crossed the brook behind my house. I crawled across a tree that was down across the brook and kept on after him. He walked all the way around Hopkins Pond, behind my house, then up the hill toward the dairy farm, then turned south and walked all the way to Blake Hill Road, crossing the road within sight of my house. When I got to that spot about 4:00 p.m., I quit and walked home, having chased that deer all day, and ending up right where I'd started! Well, I'd done a good job of tracking him, at least!

OK, so I'm still not perfect, at least when it comes to hunting. I actually gave up bowhunting because I just was not good enough at it. I seemed to shoot well in competitions at inside ranges, but I never had enough confidence to hunt deer with a bow. But I did try to hunt turkeys with the fancy expensive bow I'd purchased. I had a terrible time judging distances. I shot under and over turkeys and lost half my arrows in the process. So I went back to the shotgun.

Up ahead you'll read about more of my game mistakes. Let's hope they inspire you to do better!

Swimming for the big buck

This mistake had a happy ending. For years I had a favorite spot in the woods near the far corner of a small local pond. I could sit inside a rock formation and the deer had only a narrow pathway to go past me along the shore. There were always buck scrapes there, a sure sign that a buck will be along.

It was late November and very cold. I spotted the buck quite a ways up in the woods, and sure enough, he came right to a scrape and straddled it. He was facing me, so I waited until he turned and continued on his way to take my best shot.

I got off three shots before he bounded up and over a small knoll, running along the shore of the pond. I knew I'd hit him, so I gave him some time to lie down, then took off after him. His trail, with lots of blood, was easy to follow, but he surprised me when he turned right, moved out of the woods and into the swale grass alongside the pond.

I jumped into the grass, wandered around there, but couldn't find him. Then I raised my head and spotted him about half way across the pond. He died in the pond and was floating.

Well, I didn't know if he might sink, so I stepped back onto land and shed my clothes down to my underwear. Yes, I was not thinking very clearly at that point. I wanted to get my buck before he sank! The buck was about 150 yards out in the pond. I waded into the water, then started to swim. At about 40 yards, it finally occurred to me that this was a very bad idea. The water was freezing! And how on earth was I going to tow that buck back to shore?

Coming to my senses, I returned to shore shivering, pulled on my clothes, hiked out of the woods to my vehicle, and drove home.

My teenage son Josh helped me load the canoe and we drove to a carry-in boat launch the other end of the pond and paddled down to the buck which, much to my relief, was still floating. He had a very nice rack. We tied a rope to the antlers and towed the buck to shore. That's when I found out that the coat of a deer can absorb a lot of water. What a job we had dragging that buck up the hill to the vehicle.

If I had weighed him immediately, he'd have been a new state record! Eventually, after he dried out, I got him down to the Mount Vernon Country Store where he weighed 165 pounds. Not a state record, but certainly a buck I will never forget.

He was huge and I was shaking

I've never forgotten this buck. Even after 40 years, I can still see myself sitting on that stonewall, 30.06 in my lap, hearing him coming through the thick firs and brush, just after sunrise. A lot of the fun of hunting is the anticipation of seeing a deer, and boy, I was enjoying a lot of anticipation at that moment!

I swung left and raised my rifle, still seated, so I'd have a good shot when he stepped out of the firs, but when he did, I just lost it. He was huge! As he sauntered slowly across the 15-yard opening, I snapped off four shots without thinking. I was shaking so badly that – even though he was only about 30 yards from me – not one of those shots came close to hitting him.

Then he stopped. And I knew I had just one chance to get him. So I took a very deep breath, tried to stop shaking, peered through the scope, and fired my last shot. And I was pretty sure I'd hit him. But he bounded off, and it took me about 15 minutes to calm down and take off after him. I remember little of what happened after that. I don't think I even tried to follow his tracks. I just took off through the woods in the direction he went.

He was long gone. Morose by now, I returned to the scene and discovered a few drops of blood and a bit of hair. So I knew I'd hit him. But when I started to follow his trail, there was no blood, and eventually, no trail.

I'd never lost a wounded deer and I was so sad, walking out of the woods and to the house. Dad was there at my house, ready to join me in the day's hunt, and I told him my sad story. He suggested we go back and look some more for the buck, but I insisted it was no use, there was no blood trail, he was gone. So we drove to another favorite spot in Mount Vernon, hunted the rest of the morning, then returned to the house for lunch.

After lunch, Dad insisted that we take another look for that wounded buck, and by then I had processed all my mistakes and agreed one of them was my failure to continue looking for him. So back we went, easily picking up the buck's trail and following it for about 300 yards to a spot where he had lain down. There was lots of blood in his bed.

And now, with the two of us working on it, we were able to follow his trail as he moved toward the stream. He'd lain down once more, left more blood, and then swum across the stream. Later in the day I came up the other side of the stream but could find no trace of him. He was gone, but never forgotten, the only wounded deer I ever lost.

Postscript: I learned a lot from this experience. You just can't give up if you have hit a deer. Once, Dad and I pursued, for three days, a deer he'd wounded, and finally got the deer on the third morning.

The big buck, the tree, and me

I thought I knew every deer on my woodlot, but I'd never seen this one. After spending the afternoon hunting from the road down through my 150-acre woodlot in Mount Vernon, sitting here and there in the bog and the woods, I stepped up onto a knoll giving me a view of Hopkins Stream meandering south with about 60 minutes of hunting day left.

I heard the buck before I saw him. He was walking the shoreline, through the trees and brush, and when he stepped into view, I caught my breath. I'd never seen anything like his antlers, which looked like something you'd see on cattle, very wide, with no tines. I was kind of hidden, so I stayed put as he meandered along, turning my way and heading up the knoll right toward me.

When the buck got about half way up the knoll, he turned south again, walking slowly along, and after he passed me, I punched off the safety on my 30.06 rifle, brought it to my shoulder, and started following him in the scope. What an easy shot, I thought. I followed him for about 20 yards in the scope, until I had a perfect shoulder shot, and I took it. He was only about 50 yards away.

Glancing up, I was astonished to see him sprinting away toward the stream. I don't remember now, but I may have gotten off another shot. But I don't think so. I was so sure I'd got him with that first easy shot.

I sprinted down to the spot, saw just a few strands of deer hair, no blood, and his tracks heading toward the stream. I followed them for a short distance, coming to the place where he swam across the stream and left the area.

I couldn't believe it. It was only after I'd trudged back to the spot where I'd hit him that I noticed I'd shot right through a large oak tree. The bullet had exited the tree but couldn't have had much firepower left.

Apparently, as I focused on the deer through the scope, I had not seen the tree. Nor would I ever see that buck again, even though I pursued him across the stream, hunting that area for three days before giving up.

Erratic heart beat endangers deer hunt

Or maybe it's the other way around – the deer hunt endangers the heart. Studies have shown that the sight of a big buck can send your blood pressure and pulse skyrocketing. Actually, that might be just the remedy for my problem, an erratic and often too-slow heartbeat.

After passing out in a Gardiner restaurant on the Friday night before opening day of the firearms season on deer, I was carted to the Augusta hospital in an ambulance and captured in the cardiac unit there for the weekend. I argued strenuously, in the ambulance before it left Gardiner, that I felt much better and didn't want to go to the hospital. I knew they would never let me out in time for the next day's hunt. The ambulance attendants called my wife Linda in, showed us my EKG, and that was that. Off to the hospital we went.

For the first time in 53 years, I missed opening day. Even worse, that Sunday I was supposed to fly to North Dakota for my annual pheasant hunting trip. The guys are back now, had a terrific time, but were kind enough to say they missed me.

On Sunday the hospital cardiologist said I have sick sinus syndrome, would probably need a pacemaker, and should see my cardiologist and primary care physician the following week.

I made an appointment with each, one on Tuesday, one on Friday, and made my plans to hunt on Monday. Alas, going down to the basement of our home on Monday morning, I smelled sewerage. Never a good thing. The pipe, just outside the basement wall, had split. It took me most of that day to deal with the problem.

Tuesday morning, I got rained out. But the appointment that afternoon with Dr. Kane, my primary care doc, was reassuring. I was not in danger of heart attack or stroke. OK to go hunting. So,

103

finally, on Wednesday, I got into the woods with Dad. It was a real privilege to be hunting with him for the 53rd year. Didn't see anything that morning, but seemed to appreciate the hunt more than I ever had. Late that afternoon, in my favorite stand, a yearling buck spent 30 minutes feeding around the stand. Wonderful.

Got out again Friday morning with Harry Vanderweide and his adult daughter Amanda, who took up hunting two years ago, much to Harry's surprise. I transferred my doe permit to Amanda, hoping she'd get her first deer. We didn't see anything that morning, but they saw six deer in our other favorite spot later that day. I couldn't join them because of my appointment with my cardiologist, Dr. Lesley West.

Dr. West is awesome. She's been with me since a stent was placed in a clogged artery in 2004. That was the year of the bear referendum, and a friend noted that I seem to have these heart problems every time there is a bear referendum. Let's hope the 2014 referendum is the last one!

Dr. West was reassuring, and placed a chip in my chest to monitor fainting episodes or abnormalities in my heartbeat. Eventually, I may need a pacemaker, because my spark plug is aging and not firing as well as it should.

Feeling a whole lot better, I slept late on Saturday and got to our hunting spot too late, after Harry and Amanda had already moved on. But I decided to stay, and enjoyed a leisurely walk around this woodlot of a farmer who allows us to hunt there. Sitting high on a ridge along his back line, I watched six deer slowly walk through an opening. Two does walked into my scope, before I noticed a bigger deer coming along behind them. He was ambling along in a thicket, and I could not see his head, but I figured he was the six pointer that has been hanging with these does all week.

Even if I'd been able to confirm that, it was too long a shot, especially free hand, for me. And too early in the season to shoot a deer. And I'm focused on the big buck I know is here – I saw him twice while turkey hunting.

Don't know if my heart was racing when I spotted those deer, but I didn't faint. And I had a smile on my face throughout the long hike back to my vehicle at the end of the day. Deer hunting is most definitely good for the heart!

A lot of things can go wrong in deer hunting

I've made all the mistakes you can make in my 55 years hunting deer. I hunted throughout my teens and early twenties without even seeing a deer. In my mid twenties I began to get close enough to see some deer, and even got off occasional shots. I had a habit of walking right up to them, startled when they got up, unable to react with a rifle and scope set for a hundred-yard shot, not a hundred feet.

One cold rainy late November day, I walked a game trail in Readfield, hunting alone (no other hunter was insane enough to want to get out on this miserable day) when I spotted a rabbit about fifty feet down the trail. Taking careful aim with the 30.06, I shot the rabbit, cut through the woods about a hundred yards to put it in the trunk of my car, and returned to the spot from which I had shot.

I took about five or six steps when a large doe jumped up right beside me on the other side of a small fir. She had not moved when I shot! My wet and cold fingers couldn't even get the safety off before she was gone.

On another infamous occasion, the last day of a deerless season for both of us, Dad and I had given up and were walking out a woods road, happy in the camaraderie of a good hunting season, not really disappointed that we hadn't killed a deer, when we looked down to our left and noticed three handsome deer running along in the bottom of a ravine about 175 yards away. We stood side by side, carefully aimed, and shot the hill away just over the top of those deer.

Sometimes you don't even have to be on hand to be a victim of the cruel fates that hunting throws your way. A second deerless

105

season passed into oblivion one year as I hunted a couple of miles from home, while my wife enjoyed watching a doe meander around our front law for fifteen minutes.

Bad luck or ill timing has even caused one of my old hunting buddies, whom I will call Bigfoot, to miss some chances. Famous for his appetite, I remember one day when he left his stand and headed home for a mid-morning meal just fifteen minutes before I chased a large buck and doe right directly through where he'd been standing.

Now that I have had a lot of success hunting deer, with five big buck mounts on the wall, I wonder what changed my luck. And I marvel that I never gave up through years of adversity and bad luck. What kept me going?

Well, we are entitled in this country to life, liberty, and the pursuit of happiness. It is the pursuit of happiness that brought me into the woods and kept me there, seemingly unsuccessful in ever actually bagging a deer, but every year more and more aware of my surroundings, as well as the hunting craft and good luck that is required to consistently put venison in the freezer.

Bigfoots abound and I certainly had my own tendencies in that direction. Many hunters fail to bag a deer year after year after year. So many things can go wrong! And don't let anyone tell you that things have not gone wrong for them. We suffer together.

But few would say this is really suffering. The stories get better and better every year. The failures take on heroic proportions. The legends are built, traditions developed, crafts learned, amid the peaceful and quiet dawns and dusks of our hunting days. To all those deer we've missed before, a tip of the hat. Thanks for the memories.

To all the deer I've missed before

"To all the deer I've missed before,
Who've traveled in the great outdoors,

I'm glad they came along,
I dedicate this song,
To all the deer I've missed before."

Substituting deer for girls in this classic Willie Nelson song isn't all that farfetched. At least, it makes for a good rhyme. I dedicate this story to all those deer I've missed before.

It was a sunny day, clear and crisp. We'd hunted the lowlands in the early dawn, then planned to regroup and hit a local hunter's breakfast. As I stepped out of the woods into a field about 100 yards from the road, a huge buck stepped out of the patch of woods across the road from me.

As an instant sweat broke out on my brow and I eased off the 30.06's safety, the buck crossed the road into my field and began a slow trot across, right in front of me. In the scope, the rack appeared to have 45 to 50 points. The brute looked like a candidate for world record weight, a tiny voice whispered to me. The voice got louder and my head began to pound. As I waited for the buck to get out in front of me away from the road, St. Vidas's dance suddenly seized me. Up to that point, I hadn't even known it was in my family and genes. What a terrible time to find out!

BAM! My first shot fired across the field. The buck neither slowed nor speeded up, neither fell nor even seemed to notice this by now severely shaking orange stick figure across the field.

BAM! The second shot confirmed my worst fears. I had forgotten how to aim, indeed, my rifle, which had been so faithful for so many years, as we both awaited our first opportunity for a trophy buck, had chosen this very moment to become a stranger to me. Incredibly, we had missed again!

BAM! Now the buck was nearing yonder woods, about to disappear into the safety of the alder thicket which ringed the field, an apparition which would forever after grow into ever larger proportions in my tormented mind. But the third shot must have come close! He was turning around! He was turned around! HE WAS TROTTING BACK ACROSS THE FIELD RIGHT IN FRONT OF ME!

Having lost five pounds of liquid sweat in the past couple of minutes, I was now weak. But the rifle came shakily to the shoulder, and I carefully sighted the buck for the fourth time. He appeared to be in slow motion, gently gliding across the field no more than 100 yards from me, invincible in his grandeur.

Trying heroically to aim for the heart, I squeezed the trigger once again. Or I tried to squeeze the trigger. It was not cooperating. Just as an engine will seize up when out of oil, my mind seized up at that very moment. I blew a rod.

The gun simply wouldn't fire. Frantically I searched for the problem. I glanced up. The buck still loped along. I searched the gun some more. I glanced up again. The buck still loped along. I could not find the problem. I glanced up a third time. The buck had stopped before crossing the road and turned broadside to me. He was giving me a thorough looking over. The grin on his face should have told me of the futility of it all.

Invoking shameful words not normally part of my everyday vocabulary, I raised the gun again and sighted in. He stood there. I squeezed the unsqueezable trigger. Still no response. As I lowered the rifle, my eyes finally cleared and the fog lifted in my mind. It was the center of the storm. I looked down to see that the third bullet had failed to entirely eject, jamming the gun and preventing a fourth shell from entering the chamber.

As the buck stepped into the road I quickly cleared the chamber and jacked in the fourth shell. He was now in the road, again standing broadside gazing at me. I could not shoot. So I did the next best thing as the eye of the storm passed and I again went into a fog.

I started running toward the buck. Galloping really. In heavy hunting boots, coat, wool pants, the entire outfit. Now the buck was alerted. The bobbing orange object was coming his way. He gamely took off, still at a trot, crossing the road. I sped up. I may have even gained some ground. My breath was coming in gasps now, the legs running on adrenalin. My boot straps were loose and flying, the wool pants had dropped another six inches down the backside, and I'd lost my orange hat.

Crossing the road myself, I could still see his magnificent rack bobbing along in the deep hayfield, about 150 yards ahead, and I raised the gun to my shoulder and fired. The fourth shot was simply a shout to the heavens over the injustice of it all. It was a warning to that buck to never come back because the next time I'd be ready.

He took my advice. That huge buck, the stuff of my dreams for so many years, the first buck I'd ever encountered in the wild during the hunting season, never reappeared.

Muzzleloading hunting memories are the best

I love hunting deer with a one-shot muzzleloader. I purchased a modern in-line muzzleloader and took to the woods in the 1990s, where we often have snow during this December season and I rarely see another hunter (unless he's hunting with me). My good friend Ed Pineau and I actually try not to shoot deer in November now, so we'll have the chance to hunt in December.

Today is the opening day of the muzzleloading season, so I will share with you some of my best muzzleloading memories. And yes, my mistakes have been especially memorable!

Eight deer

I sat on a stone wall, on the higher ground, while Ed worked his way through the bog below me. This is one of our favorite strategies: one of us still hunting through an area, the other up ahead where the deer are apt to run.

I hadn't been sitting very long when I saw movement down in the woods. Imagine my astonishment when I started to count the deer, all heading my way single file: one, two, three, four, five, six, seven, eight! And the very first one was a large doe. With an any-deer permit in hand, I raised the gun, and when that doe was broadside about 40 yards away, offering a clear shot, I pulled the trigger.

And heard, "Click." Misfire. The click was loud enough that most of the deer took off, but two of them, including the one I'd picked out, went only about 30 yards and stood there while I reloaded the gun with fresh powder and aimed again at the biggest doe. And heard another, "Click." Another misfire.

I was mystified and, as you might expect, deeply disappointed. And you can imagine the ribbing I took when Ed got up to my stand and asked why I hadn't shot at any of those deer he headed my way. Actually, I'm still getting ribbed about that, years later.

But I did turn this into a learning experience. What I'd done was leave the gun, powder, and bullets out in my garage overnight, where the powder picked up some moisture. And yes, now I keep it all in the house!

Clean the gun

Two years ago, on the opening day of the muzzleloading season, I met Ed and his wife Cate at the Fayette farm where we love to hunt. Getting out of the vehicle, very excited to be kicking off this great deer hunting season, I pulled out the muzzleloader to insert the powder and bullet.

But I couldn't open the gun to insert the primer. It was stuck shut. Apparently, I'd forgotten to clean the gun at the end of the previous season. I hunted that day without a gun and then Ed loaned me one for the rest of the season. He took my gun home to see if he could get it opened and cleaned, but he couldn't. So it ended up at Audette's in Winthrop, where the guy who services their firearms got it all fixed up for me.

Another lesson learned. Clean those muzzleloaders often, and especially when the season is over!

Long shot

Ed and I have a place we reserve for muzzleloading season near the village of Wayne. It's a fairly small piece of woods near the shore of a small pond and along the stream that exits the pond. I think it was the first or second muzzleloading season when I stepped to the edge of the woods and saw a doe and large buck take off on the other side of the bog.

I raised the gun, rested it against the trunk of a large pine, and fired. A clean miss, judging by the way the deer continued to run through the swale grass. And with a muzzleloader, you only get one shot, so I was through. Later, I hiked over there just to make sure I'd missed, and I tracked the deer for a ways. No harm done.

When I met Ed later that morning, near the spot where I'd shot, I took him over to show him. "I was right here, and the buck was over there, on the far side," I said to Ed's great astonishment and amusement. "That's about 300 yards!" he exclaimed, explaining that the range of my muzzleloader was about 100 yards, tops. "You didn't even scare them," he said. Good to know and another learning experience.

The blizzard

When I got up about 4:00 a.m. that morning, it was snowing hard. Ed wasn't hunting with me that day and I thought about going back to bed. But I do love to hunt in the snow, so I bundled up and drove, very slowly and cautiously, to Wayne, where I parked on the side of the road and hiked in about 300 yards to a stone wall where I liked to sit.

The deer often cross the road here after a night of wandering and head into the bedding area near the edge of the bog. Sure enough, about a half hour after sunrise, I saw a group of deer heading my way. I could only see bits and pieces of deer, and even though I had an any-deer permit, I decided to wait for a better shot.

Unfortunately, the deer turned and headed toward a house at the top of the knoll behind me. So I turned to face that way, hoping they'd return. And after about 15 minutes, I spotted a small doe headed back down the hill toward me. When she got to about 50 yards, I fired and she dropped.

By now, it was clear this storm was going to be a blizzard. It was really snowing hard and we'd already gotten about six inches of snow. After cleaning the deer, I trudged out to my vehicle to leave my gun and backpack before returning to haul the deer out.

When I got to the road, a state trooper was parked behind my vehicle, concerned that someone had broken down. He was a bit incredulous that I was out there hunting in the blizzard, but after I told him I'd just shot a deer, he actually offered to help me haul it out! I thanked him and told him it wasn't that big and I could do it myself. And I did.

They protested my advice all over town

One year some folks in Vienna took offense to my column in *The Maine Sportsman* that recommended Vienna Mountain for deer hunting. They wanted to keep "their mountain" a secret.

Computer printed posters objecting to my column were put up throughout Mount Vernon and Vienna, encouraging people to respond by coming to my Mount Vernon house at 4:00 a.m. for a "hunters' breakfast" on opening day, and then hunting in my neighborhood. Well, Linda and I were up and ready for them, but all those muffins went to waste when no one showed up.

I didn't notice more hunters than usual in my neighborhood either. I guess that was one protest that died on the vine, or perhaps the mountaintop.

It is worth noting that regional columnists in *The Maine Sportsman* are required to cover their areas with the who, what, when, and where information. In the latter category, they are supposed to recommend prime sporting areas and include detailed directions.

For many years, I wrote those columns, and almost all of them offered specific recommendations. Suggesting Vienna Mountain to hunters was not exactly an amazing secret, because that area was very well known and popular with hunters. The insurrection even achieved a headline-grabbing story in the local daily newspaper, so the protestors actually ended up giving the mountain more publicity than my meager efforts did!

The rest of the story

I eventually gave up writing a regional column for *The Maine Sportsman*, and now write the "Capitol Report" on current issues, plus book reviews and notable quotes. And 6,000 acres, including Vienna Mountain, are now the Kennebec Highlands public lands. And yes, it's still a great place to hunt!

Wild animal tales

Fishing for a skunk in the back yard

The skunk was in the garage when Judy Dutremble of Saco, my sister-in-law, returned home from work. She opened the door and there he was, rummaging in the garbage. Judy tipped over a garbage can, leaving some garbage in it, and stood outside. Sure enough, the skunk walked right into the can, and Judy rushed up to clamp the lid on it. A quick capture! She left the skunk in the can for husband Tony to dispose of when he got home from work.

So far, not an untypical story. Skunk visits home. Skunk is captured. Skunk is removed from the premises. Well, it was in the removal that Tony established himself as a major league fisherman. Yes, that's right, I said fisherman.

Carrying the garbage can, complete with skunk, to the back yard, Tony and Judy kicked it over, expecting the skunk to emerge and make a hasty exit. With a swift kick to the can, they made their own hasty retreat to a corner of the garage and peaked around to make sure the skunk was out and on its way.

He was out all right, but the can's lid had landed right on top of him and the skunk could not get out from under that lid! The lid moved around, first to the right, then left, then back toward the house. The skunk was stuck!

Ingeniously, Tony immediately hit on a solution. Dashing into the garage, he emerged with his fishing pole with a hefty hook attached. He began "fishing" for the skunk or actually for the garbage can lid. Using his best casting technique, he threw that hook left and right, back and forth, trying to hook the lid which was by then rapidly on the move, all over the lawn, as the skunk became more and more frantic to escape his newly-acquired shell.

After about ten minutes of casting, and some very near misses, Tony incredibly made one long and graceful cast and bingo, he hooked the lid! Now I would invite you to try this in your own yard today. In fact, just place a stationary can lid about fifty feet out and try to hook it with your best casting technique. After you've failed that for 15 minutes or so, try to imagine that lid moving about with a skunk underneath. Talk about pressure!

With a solid yank, Tony pulled the hooked lid off that skunk and stood back, mopping the sweat from his brow. Then he and Judy nearly fainted as that skunk made a beeline for their neighbors' deck, promptly diving under it. Yes, the neighbor was out on the deck cooking on his gas grill, oblivious to this entire episode up to this point. The neighbor flew into high gear when Judy yelled over to him that there was a skunk under his deck. The cookout was canceled, then and there!

I nominated Tony for two special awards: Casting Champ of 1986, and membership in the Catch and Release Hall of Fame!

The unstinking pigs

In 1985, my daily newspaper trumpeted a story about loose pigs in Mount Vernon. This was my response, in a letter-to-the-editor.

Yes indeed, we've gone hog wild out here in Mount Vernon. It is always gratifying to know our daily newspaper is taking a real interest in local affairs out this way, and we're glad you appreciated the serious nature of our problem, placing it on the front page of your January 18 edition.

The headline, "Wild Hogs Cause Stink," was somewhat incorrect, however, because pigs do not stink. They're very neat and clean actually. But you city slickers wouldn't be expected to know that.

We do have other equally serious problems which you may be interested in covering now that you've discovered our potential for splashy news stories. Property taxes are threatening to get out of hand, for instance, and we have at least one unusual approach to solving this pesky problem.

Taking note that the Fish and Wildlife Department made a whopping $600,000 on this year's state duck stamp, we're considering issuing a town pig stamp, and sponsoring a limited one-week hunt at the end of February. We'll be real tired of those loose pigs by then, and they might's well help some needy families get through the rest of a tough winter.

We'd be interested to know what you city folks think of this idea. Would you be interested in hunting pigs? Or would you buy the pig stamp just to add to your stamp collections? What's the going rate for these things?

To keep the interest up, we've arranged another story for you next week. We've asked Ray Hall to loose some cows, and they'll be stampeding through the village at 2:00 p.m. Wednesday afternoon. Please station your reporter and photographer in the middle of the intersection in front of the country store. You'll get a real fine close-up photo for Thursday's front page.

Our rescue squad will be on hand to administer assistance should your people get too much of a close-up. Looking forward to seeing you on Wednesday. - George A. Smith, Selectman, Mount Vernon

Battling wildlife in the home

Last week I wrote about Jim Sterba's book, *Nature Wars*, that offers a fascinating look at out-of-control populations of wildlife, explains why this has happened, and relates many backyard battles with a variety of critters from deer to beaver. Sterba neglected one crucial aspect of this problem, when the battles move into the home.

And I'm not just talking about mice, although we've done battle with plenty of them. One winter I caught 38, an even dozen of them trapped in a kitchen drawer. And this doesn't count the mice our cat killed. Often we wake in the middle of the night to a commotion in the dining room outside our bedroom door, as the cat and his quarry careen around the room. Sometimes I have to get up and stomp the mouse to death. My stomping record is eight, in a two-week period.

Bats are a particular challenge. In the early years, I'd try to kill them with a fireplace poker. For years there was a hole in our kitchen ceiling where I once missed a bat with the poker. Since getting educated to the benefits bats bring to the neighborhood, and worried about their diminishing populations, I now catch them in a long-handled fishing net, gently releasing them outside.

Then there is the snake episode. Linda hates snakes. One day as she was washing the kitchen floor, she moved a wicker basket that I'd left outside for some time the day before, and a large snake slithered out of the bottom of the basket.

She grabbed the fireplace shovel and jumped up on a kitchen chair, gradually bludgeoning the harmless thing to death. At one point in this fierce battle, she called me. All I could do was encourage her to keep at it. She was still shook up when I got home and still shudders when I bring up the incident.

Every wild critter that can get into the house, does so. Red squirrels are particularly nettlesome. I watch for them at the bird feeder, and if they turn toward the house after dining, I shoot them. If they head for the woods, they get a reprieve. A chipmunk currently resides in my workshop and the garage, darting into a tunnel under the cement floor when he sees me.

One sunny Saturday morning, I opened the bulkhead door to air out the cellar. A bit later, heading out of the cellar up the bulkhead's steps, I met a huge raccoon coming down the steps. We had a stare down, and he eventually reversed course. I'm not sure what would have happened if he'd continued down the steps. He was certainly too big to stomp to death.

And then there is the night I woke to a terrible ruckus directly below my pillow, under the bed. Turned out to be mating raccoons.

One morning Lin exited the bedroom to find a chickadee sitting on her computer, apparently brought into the house by the cat. Another time, the cat brought in a sparrow. Lin yelled at the cat and he dropped the bird. It promptly lifted off and flew into my office. Lin put on a pair of gloves and chased the bird around the room, finally catching and setting it outside. Not all wildlife-in-the-home stories have a bad ending.

But some of these encounters are frightening, especially the rabid fox that entered our garage while I was out of town. Lin called the local game warden and he came and shot it. Our dog, chained in the front yard, had to be quarantined for a while, even though we weren't sure it got near the fox. All was well that ended well.

And I guess that's the message here. Choosing to live in and around their homes, we must expect, occasionally, that these wild critters will like our homes. Some we can live with. Some not so much.

Nature at peace

Woodchucks are one of the few wild critters Linda allows me to shoot in the yard. Anything that gets into her garden is fair game. This season, I shot two fat chucks, but a smaller one eluded me. Our cats would chase it around but never catch it.

Then our neighbor Dona came through. One week when we were at camp, she captured the woodchuck in a live trap and, kind soul that she is, transported it far away where it could live in the forest without annoying any home gardener – at least that was the theory.

We had two blissful weeks of harvesting Lin's prolific garden without competition, when I heard a knock on the door and opened it to find our young neighbor, Justin Brickett, and his beagle. Always polite, Justin said, "Mr. Smith, I just saw a Bald Eagle flying up the road with a woodchuck. The woodchuck was heavy and the eagle dropped it in the bushes near your lawn."

Great. Now we've got eagles delivering woodchucks to us. Of course, the woodchuck did have a bad day and it might not have survived the ordeal, but Justin and I couldn't find it in the bushes.

Whenever I encounter the "eat or be eaten" situation that exists in the wilds of Maine, I am reminded of conversations with Buzz Caverly, the executive director of Baxter State Park, who often described the park as "nature at peace." Nature is rarely at peace. It's a killing field out there.

Daughter Rebekah was at our camp on the edge of Baxter Park a few weeks ago, when she heard screeching one night. Outside, she saw a huge great horned owl killing a rabbit on the lawn in front of camp. The owl flew up into a nearby tree and waited patiently for Becky to go back inside so he could enjoy his meal.

The next week, Linda and I found a baby bunny living in the woodpile beside our camp's fire pit on the front lawn. The bunny would come out during the day and lie in the grass next to the woodpile. Lin laid out a scrumptious meal for the bunny one day, but he chose to ignore it. He appeared to be healthy.

118

The morning we were to leave for home, Lin looked out the camp's front window and saw a large coyote sniffing around the woodpile, hoping for a breakfast bunny. We chased the coyote away, although he took his time and kept looking back wistfully in the direction of the woodpile. No doubt he was back soon after we left. That bunny didn't have a chance. We never saw it again.

We accept this, in the wilds. It's only when the wild critters invade what we consider our space that we really take notice. Rep. Mike Shaw, a Democrat from Standish, told me last spring that a weasel had gotten into his hen house and killed 45 chicks in one night, hauling them under the floor. The tiny weasel is a killing machine.

One Thanksgiving morning during a blizzard, we looked out the front kitchen window of our Mount Vernon home just in time to see a sharp shinned hawk knock a blue jay off the feeder and to the ground. The hawk pecked away rapidly at the jay, blue feathers flying in all directions. Lin couldn't watch. I of course was fascinated. Those blue feathers, flying up and into the cascading white snow, were kind of beautiful.

Over the years I have witnessed astonishing carnage in the fields and forests of Maine and beyond. One day while golfing in Florida, I saw a largemouth bass come right out of the water to snare a small bird.

For years, I hated snapping turtles after seeing one take a baby duck off the surface of the pond behind our house. Sportsmen hate coyotes that haul down deer and start cruelly chewing on them while they're still alive.

But I've often enjoyed watching foxes "mousing" in the fields. They stalk quietly along in the tall grass, then jump high and pounce on the unsuspecting mouse. Of course, while I enjoy the spectacle, it's not so good for the mouse. In Labrador, we fished with imitations of mice and voles, skittering them across the surface of the river until huge brook trout grabbed them. The trout up there eat a lot of voles that fall into the river.

A few years ago a woman in the Millinocket area captured on video a bear grabbing and lugging off a moose calf. All she could do was scream, "It's killing the baby! It's killing the baby!"

Ah, yes, but that's nature at peace.

Wildlife watching

The weasel ran up my leg and chest and could have killed me! Sitting on the ground one November afternoon, leaning up against a big pine tree, I was anticipating a deer coming out of a bedding area nearby, when I spotted a weasel dashing back and forth about 40 yards away. Suddenly, the weasel turned toward me and sprinted in my direction.

Before I could react, he raced up my leg and chest, where he stopped to assess the situation. Weasels are killing machines, and I thought later that if he'd bitten my neck, I could have died. Fortunately, he decided I was not the pine tree he expected, and he jumped from my chest and took off.

Bob Duchesne, in a presentation to this year's annual meeting of the Small Woodland Owners Association of Maine, reported that a national study found that 57% of Mainers enjoy watching wildlife, more than the citizens of any other state. The percentage surprised me, because don't we all love to see our state's wild critters? Well, I guess not when they are running up your leg and chest!

I've probably had more encounters with wildlife than many folks, given the time I spend outdoors in the woods and on the waters of our state. Here are some of my more memorable encounters.

Raccoons

When I told Linda this morning that I was writing this column, she noted that, "There's something to be said for sitting here by our picture window every morning watching the birds. You learn a lot." And she's right about that, but her statement reminded me of the time she got aggravated when a raccoon climbed up the metal pole holding one of her feeders and cleaned it out every night.

So one afternoon, she went out and sprayed the pole with Pam. About an hour after dark that night, we spotted the raccoon approaching the house. Standing at the kitchen window, we watched as the coon climbed a short ways up the pole, then slid back down. He repeated that four times, then stood on the ground and turned toward us as if to say, "Now, what did you do?" As he sauntered back across the lawn toward the woods, I could almost feel his disappointment.

Foxes

Before we contracted with Modern Pest Management for boxes of poison that substantially reduced the number of mice living with us, I would catch them and toss them into the bushes beside the house. After a while, I noticed that a fox, on a regular basis, would emerge from the woods and trot right over to that spot where I was tossing the mice.

We had a tame fox at camp one summer. He'd come around on a regular basis, and hang out with us. And at home one year, a fox would often climb up and lie in the bench beside our front door. Sometimes we'd drive in and spot the fox, snoozing there.

Coyotes

Coyotes are a controversial critter, for sure, especially with deer hunters who know that coyotes kill a lot of deer. But they can also be very entertaining. I see them every so often in and around my woodlot, and hear them howling at night, and we've even seen them on the front lawn. Last year coyotes killed a deer right next to the fenced in area holding our neighbor's horses.

There's a bunch of big boulders on my neighbor's woodlot, where porcupines typically gathered, but one fall, I found a dead coyote lying in one of the holes under the boulder. I've no idea what killed the coyote.

Dad, Harry Vanderweide, and I were sitting in the dark one day in Windsor, calling to turkeys in the nearby trees, when we were surprised by a coyote that jumped out of the nearby brush and right onto one of our turkey decoys. He didn't stay around long, figuring out quickly that the decoy was not going to be anything he wanted to eat. This actually happened twice that year.

One spring I was sitting behind a rock wall, with my decoys out in front of me in a field, when I spotted a beautiful golden-coated coyote trotting down the field toward my decoys. He circled the decoys, realizing they weren't real turkeys, and then trotted back up the field and into the woods. I made the mistake of writing about this in my outdoor news blog, and got roasted by some readers for not shooting the coyote.

Skunks

Skunks dig up our lawn on a regular basis, and I don't mess with them unless they become a real nuisance. One evening we came home and found our cat at the front door, dripping some kind of liquid from his face. And it wasn't hard to figure out what had happened to him. What a stench! He'd gotten blasted right in the face by a skunk. That might be why he won't go out at night anymore!

I know just how he felt. Running a bit late for a selectmen's meeting one evening years ago, I dashed down the stairs into my workshop without turning on the light. Approaching the door to the garage, I felt our cat move across my feet in front of me and reached down to pet him. Bad mistake.

The skunk blasted me right in the face, and I staggered and started running back upstairs, shedding my stinking clothing along the way before jumping into the shower. Linda later collected the clothing and threw it away. Eventually I got to the selectmen's meeting. No one sat near me.

Bears

It's always exciting to see a bear – but most of the time, you see the hind end as the bear runs away. Unless of course the bear is a sow with cubs. Then they can be very dangerous. Time for you to back away!

I found a bear's den one winter up in the Kennebec Highlands, 10 minutes from our house, and bears have been seen occasionally throughout our town of Mount Vernon. I've seen many bears in western and northern Maine.

One year I was driving out of the woods after fishing a stream north of Rangeley when two cubs ran across the road and up into a tree followed closely by their mom, who stopped behind a downed tree. We couldn't see her but she was tearing up the area and roaring, and my friend was in a panic, because I'd stopped the vehicle to take photos of the cubs.

I could do that without getting out of the vehicle, but my friend was still going nuts, eager to get out of there. I will admit, the sow sounded ferocious! But we escaped, with a few nice photos and a memorable encounter.

At our camp on Sourdnahunk Lake, next to Baxter State Park, we often see bears. One of our most memorable encounters was when our kids were small. We were all returning to camp after a walk, coming up the driveway to our camp, when we saw a bear sauntering toward us, also in the driveway. The bear stopped, looked at us, and turned left into the woods. Pretty soon we heard it moving through the woods to our right, and – Surprise! – it popped out into the driveway about 50 yards beyond us, continuing on its way with just a slight detour around us.

Another time, I was walking Baxter Park's perimeter road near our camp, when I saw a bear coming up through the woods, headed right toward me. I backed up and picked up a rock, just in case. If the bear continued on its route, it would pop out into the road about 30 yards in front of me. But just before it got to the road, it turned my way and started walking just off the road, coming right at me. I figured that was enough of that, and hollered. The bear stopped quickly, looked up, turned, and bounded away. I can still see it whirling around and sprinting off.

One day I was fishing a remote stream in Baxter Park, when I rounded a bend and heard growling and shrieking up ahead in the alders, which were swaying this way and that. I thought it was a bear, killing a moose calf or deer. So I moved onto a small island in the stream, and tried to see them. I couldn't do that, but the racket went on for quite some time, when they suddenly left.

They crossed the stream around the next bend, out of my sight, then started back upstream in woods toward me. And that's when I beat a hasty retreat, heading back up stream and returning to camp.

When I got home, I called a wildlife biologist at the Department of Inland Fisheries and Wildlife, and after I described what I saw and heard, he told me it would have been mating bears – and that I was very wise to have retreated!

Our absolutely most memorable experience also happened at camp. Another camp owner raced up the hill to our camp to alert us to a bear that was swimming across the lake, headed toward our camp. We grabbed a camera and ran down to the shore. The bear was only a couple hundred feet out in the lake by that time, and we were very surprised to see a cub on the sow's back and a second cub swimming behind her. She may have seen us because she turned slightly and came ashore on the other side of a stream that enters the lake at our camp. She stopped on the shore to shake off some water, and we got great photos of both the sow and her cubs, before they moved off into the alders.

Beaver

Beaver can be destructive, but fun. We have four beaver houses on Hopkins Stream that passes by our house. We had two relatively new apple trees on our front lawn one year, and when I went out to get the morning newspaper, I did a double-take. One tree was completely gone – a tasty treat for the family of beaver living on the stream. That year I put metal pieces around the trees I wanted to save, and that did the trick.

Beaver love apples, but they're not smart. After they eat the apples, they also eat the tree! If you look carefully, every fall you'll see a beaten down path from the stream across our side lawn to the apple trees, where the beavers chow down. One evening I pulled into the driveway and my vehicle's lights lit up a huge beaver in the driveway with a big red apple in his mouth. Wish I'd gotten a photo of that!

Beaver are not great at sharing their space either. Quite often, fishing a favorite stream up near camp, a beaver will come out of its house to slap the water with its tail, a warning to me to get out of their water. One time I was standing in the stream where a small beaver dam had created a nice pond full of trout, when a beaver came out of its house, slamming its tail on the water. When I didn't immediately retreat, it dived and headed for me. I could see it coming. Not sure of what it planned to do to me, I quickly retreated up stream.

A few years ago beaver moved into the bog on my woodlot and built a dam on a tiny brook, completely flooding the bog and making it hard for me to get through it and to hunt there. I asked a friend to trap beaver there that winter, and he caught several small beaver, but no large ones. The flooded water now covers a huge area, so I asked my trapper friend to return this winter. On a scouting mission a few weeks ago, he reported that he'd seen no sign that beaver were still there, and recommended that I breach the dam and drain the water. I'm going to do that soon.

In the winter, I like to snowshoe up to a beaver house and listen to them talking inside. You can actually hear them, by listening at the air hole in their house.

Bobcats

Bobcats are shy elusive animals, so you don't often see them. But they are plentiful throughout the state. I've only seen them a couple of times on my woodlot, but notice their tracks almost every time I snowshoe there.

One winter in our back yard, at the bottom of a large apple tree, I found the feathers of a turkey along with bobcat tracks. From the snow, I could tell that quite a ruckus had happened there. Turns out the bobcat had sat in the crotch of the tree, and when the turkey had walked by, the cat jumped on it and killed it, dragging it about 20 yards back into the woods and eating most of it.

Porcupines

The Dairy of Daniel E. Heywood: A Parmachenee Guide at Camp Caribou, Parmachenee Lake (1891) (a Legacy Reprint from Kessinger Publishing) is a fascinating account of hunting and trapping above Rangeley in 1891. It includes this story about porcupines (hedgehogs):

I once saw a hedgehog swimming in the lake and killed it. It had crossed from an island one-fourth mile distant, and was near the shore when I saw it. I never knew any good to come from a hedgehog, and there is no end to the trouble which comes from them in localities where they are plenty. Besides their quills and their gnawing of articles left around camps, one hedgehog will reduce a shade tree to ruin, be it poplar, elm, birch, maple, beech or any other hardwood tree, in one night; therefore I always expend the contents of my revolver on one, wherever I meet it, and think I take no charms from these woods by doing.

I do the same thing! I once had a dog that just never learned. Several times I had to pull quills out of him, until one day he got a big load of them in his mouth and I had to take him to the vet to get them extracted. Because they are so destructive to trees, I usually shoot them if I see them in the yard or on my woodlot. There's a group of big boulders there where porcupines live in the crevices underneath the boulders, and I often find them in the trees nearby.

This fall, I saw a porcupine on the front lawn, hunkered down next to one of our apple trees, so I loaded a shell into my .22 rifle and walked right up to it, aimed for the back of its head, and shot it. Imagine my amazement when it sauntered away, crossed the road, and continued on into the woods. Yes, they are some old tough!

Snapping turtles

Snapping turtles kill and eat a lot of young ducklings and loons. And they can be nasty when encountered in the water. A huge one chased me right out of the brook behind my house one day when I was fishing there. We seem to have a lot of snappers around my house. They lay their eggs along the road, or often in Linda's flower and vegetable gardens. For years, when I saw them laying eggs along the road, I would run over them.

Then I smartened up, redeeming myself somewhat one time when Linda and I were returning home during an evening rain storm, and found a bunch of baby snappers on the bridge in front of our house. Many had been run over. I got out and carefully sought out all those that were still alive, and carried them across the road to the shore of the stream.

But Linda still doesn't care for them when they get into her garden. A few years ago she saw one out back in the vegetable garden, so she scooted it into a shovel and carried it far back into the woods. An hour later, she looked up to see it emerging from the woods, headed back to the garden!

Fishers

Fishers love cats. Well, they love to eat cats. If a cat disappears in your neighborhood, the prime suspect should be a fisher. One year a distraught neighbor called. A fisher had cornered her cat in the basement of their home. She discovered this in the nick of time and was able to scare the fisher away, but she wanted to know what could be done.

I called a local trapper who set some traps in the area, and caught several fishers – all females. Two were caught on my woodlot right across the road from the lady's house. But there are still fisher out there, and I often see their tracks, particularly in the winter.

One November day when I was deer hunting, a pair of fisher came bounding along through the woods. It was the first time I'd see a male fisher. Boy, they are huge! When they got to me, both fishers climbed a tree and sat there looking at me. Eventually, they climbed down and took off.

Up to camp, I once caught a bat while fly fishing. I had just cast and the bat swept down and grabbed my fly right in the air, hooking itself. I reeled it in, lifted it into the boat, and carefully released it. Yes, I practice catch and release!

A saw whet owl got stuck in our garage once, and knocked itself out trying to escape. I discovered it, picked it up, held it for a while, and when it came to, released it outside.

Birding

Linda and I started bird watching about 12 years ago, after seeing our neighbor Dona Seegers in our front yard with binoculars. The first time I saw a Blackburnian Warbler, I was hooked. We graduated from bird watchers to birders when we started traveling, just to see birds. With four birding trips to Texas, one to Arizona, and one to Costa Rica, I guess you could say we are hooked. We even spend some of our time in Italy birding.

One time, we spotted a beautiful bird along the stream that runs through the Italian village of Greve. It was bright yellow with a red head. We raced back to our apartment to look it up in our bird book, and were surprised to find it was a European Goldfinch. And the first time we saw a Hoophoe – well, Wow! What a magnificent bird!

We spend a weekend in May on Monhegan Island every year, where sometimes the migrating birds are so tired they are all sitting on the ground. Up to camp, we love seeing unusual birds like Spruce Grouse and Borial Chickadees.

Every August finds us in Lubec, birding on the South Lubec sandbar within sight of the place where my mom grew up and only a short distance from West Quoddy Head lighthouse where my grandfather Ephraim Johnson kept the light for three decades.

Maine's top birding guide and author of the *Maine Birding Trail*, Bob Duchesne says the sandbar is the best place in Maine to see migrating shorebirds and he does not exaggerate. The Nature Conservancy purchased the sandbar and it is now in the ownership of the Department of Inland Fisheries and Wildlife. But the birds rent space there, by the thousands, from early August to mid-September, on their way south.

We spot an amazing array of shorebirds there. I wished so much my mother was alive so I could ask her: Did you know what an amazing place this is when you were growing up here? Did you notice all these birds?

Loons

Loons often nest in the swale grass along Hopkins Stream. When paddling downstream, we give them a wide berth.

Linda and I were working in the garden one afternoon when we heard a voice hollering from the woods. I thought I heard, "I've got a loon and need help." That didn't make a lot of sense to me, but sure enough, when I stepped into the woods, there was Shearon Murphy with a loon cradled under her arm. And here is that loon's story.

Jane Naliboff photographed the loon the morning of September 7 on Minnehonk Lake. When she got home and loaded the photos into her computer, something looked very wrong. So she emailed the photos to Keel Kemper, a wildlife biologist with Maine's Department of Inland Fisheries and Wildlife.

Keel agreed that something was wrong with the loon and recommended a rescue. Jane contacted Avian Haven, and late that afternoon, Shearon Murphy, a volunteer waterfowl rescuer, showed up with her kayak, paddled out to the loon, now in the outlet of the lake right behind our Mount Vernon home, and simply reached down and picked up the loon. Definitely not something that would ever happen with a healthy loon.

Looking into the right eye of that beautiful creature, I too knew that something was very, very wrong. The loon's head and neck languished on Shearon's hip as I drove her back to her vehicle, where Jane met us, along with Barbara Skapa who had joined in the rescue mission. We loaded the loon into a box, covered it up with a sheet I'd grabbed from our garage, and Shearon took off to deliver the loon to Avian Haven, where a large lead sinker was found in its gizzard.

The next day, Jane published her story and lots of photos in the *Daily Bulldog*, reporting, "The good news is that after lavage (pouring water into the gizzard to flush out the sinker), it worked. The sinker came out! It's now getting chelation therapy to lower the lead level to a normal range. When that happens, it will be released back to its natural environment. It's a happy ending for what was almost another dead water bird due to human behavior."

Boy, I was some old happy to read this and pleased with the small role I played in the rescue of this beautiful creature. Alas, at 9:00 p.m. that night, Jane posted this: "It is with great sadness and disappointment that I must tell you: despite a successful lavage procedure, our friend survived only a few more hours before succumbing to lead poisoning. Everyone did all they could, and we are all heartbroken."

This tragedy led me to help a coalition of groups led by Maine Audubon to ban lead sinkers and fishing lures. We're not there yet, but we've banned the worst of them.

For birds, it's all about habitat. You might think our front yard is a bit scraggly. I used to keep it neat, cutting all the brush, but then I learned that the brush was great habitat for birds – including the yellow warblers that nest in those bushes to the left of our front door.

Fishing for birds

I knew I was hooked on birding one year when Harry Vanderweide and I were on a very remote lake in Quebec, fishing for native brook trout, when I asked Harry to reel up his line because I wanted to motor over to a nearby island where I'd spotted a flock of very interesting birds.

Harry should have been prepared for that, because we had been turkey hunting earlier that year when I left our turkey blind to identify a bird I'd heard singing in the woods behind us.

If you'd ever sat in a canoe, fishing, and seen an osprey dive straight down into the pond, creating a big splash, and emerging with a fish – well, you'd never forget it. I especially enjoy our neighborhood Bald Eagles who often sit in a tall pine, on the edge of Hopkins Pond, where I can watch them from my office window.

Bird watching is a wonderful hobby. All you need is an inexpensive pair of binoculars and a bird book. And when you see your first warbler, you'll be hooked.

* * *

It's always exciting to see deer and moose. But after we purchased our camp in the north woods, at Camp Phoenix, we saw so many moose that our young daughter Hilary wouldn't even look up when we said, "Hey, look, there's a moose!" Moose surrounded us at camp, oftentimes seen right on the lawn.

One old cow had only one eye, so of course we called her One-Eye, and she had a calf every year for many years. We've got a photo of One-Eye in the camp library. Eventually she disappeared, and we figured she'd died.

One time another camp owner looked out his kitchen window and saw a bear stalking a moose calf, while the mother moose was in the beaver pond on our property. He rushed out and got the bear's attention, and the bear came his way. He ended up in the back of his truck, while the bear leaned on the fender and looked in. The cow moose took notice and scampered away with her calf. It took a while for the bear to leave the premises, but our friend accomplished his mission, none the worse for the wear.

We had a canoe stashed at one remote pond near camp, and could always count on seeing a lot of moose in the water there in August. One year, there was an old bull with a withered set of antlers up at the far end of the pond, so we paddled up to see him. He'd dip his head under water, eating plants, then pop back up. His head was crowded with flies that would hover over the water every time he dipped his head under water.

As we approached and his head disappeared under water, I got too close and those flies – hundreds of them – moved over and settled on me. Linda and the kids were in the canoe, but all the flies surrounded me. I paddled furiously all over the pond, trying to get rid of them. Ouch!

Linda and I often saw moose when we walked the Perimeter Road in Baxter Park, right behind our camp. One time, we were following a cow when a truck came down the road, headed our way, and the cow turned quickly and galloped in our direction. We had just time enough to jump into the woods, and she whipped past us no more than ten feet away.

Hunting through the bog on my woodlot in Mount Vernon one afternoon, I heard a moose calf bleating, and then, suddenly, the cow burst out of the bushes headed right my way, kicking up her heels. All I had time to do was dive to the right into the bushes, and she blasted by me, no more than five feet away, still kicking. Close call!

From one of my deer hunting stands on my woodlot, I often saw moose, three young bulls one time, a huge old bull another time. That huge bull knew there was something in the tree, and he walked over to my stand and looked up at me, his antlers right even with my feet. Exciting!

Alas, moose seemed to have disappeared around our house. The last one we saw was five years ago, a young one. Up to camp, it's equally discouraging. Last August I took our daughter Hilary's boyfriend, who had never seen a moose, to all the usual places where we could always see moose in August, and I couldn't find one.

Deer

We see lots of deer on our lawn in Mount Vernon and had to put up electric fence to keep them out of the garden. But it's up to camp where we've most enjoyed them.

Deer were always around camp, often on the lawn. One year a doe dropped her fawn right in the deep grass on our lawn. We got photos, of course. Another year, a doe would join the kids out back in a whiffle ball game. I always wondered if she thought the whiffle ball was a salt lick. I have photos of her nosing the ball, while playing first base. Yes, she liked to play first base!

For several years, a doe at Sourdnahunk Lake had triplets and we got photos of them, a beautiful sight. Alas, the deer herd in the north woods has also declined significantly, and we didn't see a single deer last summer up there, not a one.

133

Fishing favorites

The charm of fishing is that it is the pursuit of what is elusive but attainable. A perpetual series of occasions for hope. – John Buchan

First fishing memories

Spring fishing would officially get underway when Dad announced at the supper table that the family would go perch fishing that evening down to the Waugan. Or sometimes it was up to Dead Stream. No matter. The white perch were spawning everywhere, and voracious.

The young boy knew his Dad liked to get in the boat and troll, but that was too slow for a youngster who measured his time in minutes and packed a lot into each 60 seconds. When Dad mentioned perch, the rods and reels would come out quickly and the spade would be put to work in the garden, Dad turning over the soil while the boy mined that soil for angler worms. The pail came out, ready to fill up with perch, and they were off.

Dad didn't usually get his line into the water. He was kept busy helping the boy. Casting was something the boy had yet to master, and there was often a tangled confusion in getting the job done. Then there was the madly flopping fish to deal with, rearming the hook with a new worm, and lots of other things to attend to as well.

Dad never seemed to mind though. And the boy was too busy and excited to notice who was catching all the fish. When they got home Dad cleaned all the fish while the boy "helped." It would be years before his help was really helpful. But these were his first fishing memories. Thanks Dad!

These fishing tales are all true!

I started fishing at a very young age, thanks to Dad, and have enjoyed introducing my children and grandchildren to fishing. My kids caught buckets of spawning white perch, at the inlet to Maranacook Lake, the same place I caught buckets of white perch when I was a kid. I can still see the kids' bobbers popping up and down, and Josh and Hilary screaming, in tandem, "I got one!" The swift retrieve, little hands winding the Zebco for all it's worth. That was real fishing!

At the Maranacook inlet, crowds hugged the shore, a half-dozen bobbers clung to the electric wires overhead, and chaos reigned when the perch were running. It was strictly hook, line, and bobber, with nothing as productive as a succulent garden worm. My role was official wormer, inserting the hooks into those juicy worms.

At the age of seven, Josh was casting well, but 4-year-old Hilary wasn't quite ready, so I cast for her. But make no mistake – she didn't need help reeling in those fish. Any offer from me in that regard was swiftly turned aside with a firm, "I can do it myself, Dad."

As we reached our personal limit of a dozen fish for dinner, Hilary's interest turned to the perch still flopping around in our large bucket. "Will you shoot them when we get home, Dad?" she asked. I explained that shooting would not be necessary!

Camp

Both son Josh and daughter Hilary learned to tie flies at our North Woods camp. Josh specialized in a secret fly that always caught more fish at camp than any other fly. He still makes those for me at Christmas. Hilary refused to tie any ordinary fly. Her flies were always very colorful and creative. I have a photo of Hil with the first brook trout she ever caught on a fly she tied. We'd gone to a favorite spot on Sourdnahunk Stream, where I'd carried her on my back across the stream so she could fish a favorite pool. And she caught a trout immediately, on a very colorful red and blue fly. That's one of my favorite photos and is still displayed in my home office.

Grandson Vishal is my latest fishing buddy. Actually, V is a fishing machine. Hoping to teach him how to cast an open-faced reel one year, I took him to the shore of the lake near his home, took two casts to demonstrate how to do it, and was preparing to cast again when V said, "Grampy, let me try it." So I handed him the rod and he threw that lure way out into the lake, as if he'd been casting for years.

When he was eight, we were fishing a remote pond near my home on a rainy day, and after he'd reeled in about two dozen small bass, I told him it was time to head home, but that he could keep fishing while I paddled the canoe over to the landing. I'd paddled only about 50 yards when I looked over and his face was covered in a huge smile, his rod bent double. Fish on! V worked the bass in like a pro, and it was the biggest bass I'd ever seen come out of that pond, about three pounds. Another memorable day on the water.

I turned the tables on Dad when we purchased our camp on Sourdnahunk Lake, which is fly fishing only. Dad had never fly fished, but he gamely gave it a try, never quite mastering the casting technique, but doing well enough to catch fish. We had many memorable evenings fishing at camp. One time a loon grabbed his trout as he was reeling it in, and wouldn't let go. When Dad got the fish to the boat, he gave the line a yank and the trout came out of the loon's mouth. That loon was mighty unhappy! He swam all around the boat, flapping his wings and screeching at us.

Dad liked to get up early to fish, unlike his son, and one day I'd just arisen when he sauntered up from the shore and stepped into camp. "How'd you do, Dad?" I asked. "Oh, ok, I guess," he said. "I caught one." He'd left the trout on the porch, so I went out to take a look. And I was stunned. It was a very fat 16-inch trout, the biggest we'd ever caught at camp!

While anglers are allowed a certain amount of exaggeration in their stories, especially as the years go on, the stories in this book are all true. I swear.

Dad breaks out of hospice to catch trout

It's no accident that much of my career was spent as an advocate for Maine sportsmen, or that I am now writing outdoor news and for 13 years cohosted a TV show focused on hunting, fishing, and conservation and environmental issues. My Dad, Ezra Smith of Winthrop, set me on this course from birth. In 2013 Dad and I hunted together for the 53rd year, a wonderful privilege for me. I guess we must have fished together for 60 years.

But Dad is now in the Hospice Unit at the Togus V.A., with serious health problems. He is actually thriving there, thanks to the wonderful professional staff and amazing volunteers. We've set up a corner of his room with his painting supplies, and he's doing a lot of painting. His room is stuffed with his paintings and carvings, and last week he had me bring in his keyboard so he could play some music.

And I've gotten him out five times to fish for brook trout. On the Togus campus, in a small pond created by a dam on the stream that passes through there, he's been catching brook trout – right in the middle of some hot sunny summer days. The first visit, I told Dad not to expect to catch anything, trout don't bite on beautiful sunny afternoons, and he promptly hauled one in.

Monday of this week was the first time he got skunked, but as he told the staff at the Hospice Unit when we returned, it was good fishing, poor catching. He didn't seem at all disappointed. All of the fish were returned to the water, except one we accidentally killed. Dad's lady friend Irma got to take that one home for supper.

If you ever feel you might not be getting your money's worth from your Maine fishing license, consider this. Maine's Department of Inland Fisheries and Wildlife stocks that Togus pond with brook trout for the patients at the hospital and in the other units. Only the patients are allowed to fish there.

I wheel Dad out to the Subaru in his wheelchair, drive over to the pond, wheel him out to the edge of the water, in a nice shady spot, and hand him his light spinning rod. Sitting there, watching him cast, is worth a whole lot more than I paid for my fishing license. And every cast represents a parcel of wonderful memories.

Nothing finer than family fishing

As I cast a Brown Wulff to a Sourdnahunk Lake brook trout that had risen about 40 feet from the boat, I was startled by a shout from young Joshua at the other end of the boat.

"I got him!" he exclaimed. The water about six feet in front of me erupted as Josh's brookie fought to separate himself from my son's Hornberg. Josh had spotted the trout's rise right beside the boat while my eyes were looking much further out, and he had carefully dropped his own fly into the middle of the ring.

The fish struck immediately and Josh professionally set the hook. Up went his rod just as we had practiced, and the battle was on. Keeping a tight line, Josh played the fish well, bringing it in quickly so as not to tire it needlessly if we decided to release it.

But I took one look at that brookie boatside and knew it was a keeper. Josh has released his share of fish and he deserved this one. I dropped it out of the net into the bottom of the boat and almost in unison our two voices said, "Wow, what a fish!" It was Josh's biggest fish to date, a colorful and fat 13-inch brook trout. It perfectly matched a fish I'd caught earlier that evening, and we limited our catch to those two fish, releasing the rest that evening.

If there's a bigger thrill for a twelve-year-old than casting a dry fly and catching a hefty 13-inch native brook trout in the shadow of Mount Katahdin, I guess I don't know what it is. Heck, it's a pretty big thrill for me, watching my son working that rod and bringing in that trout.

I'm doubly blessed because my nine-year-old daughter is an avid angler too. Earlier that week, Hilary joined Josh in a small boat they paddle around a nearby beaver pond. Josh fashioned a rod for her from a nearby alder branch and attached about six feet of thread to it, at the end of which he tied on a small dry fly, part of his collection of old flies that his grandfather purchased for him at a yard sale. Hilary didn't hook any trout in the pond with that rod, but she hooked herself on fly fishing. After that, I couldn't keep her out of the boat! And she adored her alder branch rod, which still hangs on the wall at camp.

A day later we traveled to a nearby brook with our respective fly rods. We scampered from the Baxter Park perimeter road down a steep bank to the brook's edge where I waded the stream carrying Hilary on my back to the other side. Eventually I placed her, still fishing her alder branch with thread and dry fly, in the middle of the brook, perched on a downed tree, so she could fish a deep hole that I was certain held some trout.

She began getting strikes immediately and fished intently for over an hour, trying to hook those tiny trout, none of which go more than six inches. She never hooked one, but she got more strikes with that foolish alder branch than I did with my $150 LL Bean fly rod.

Later that week, Josh and I fished the evening Mayfly hatch in a stiff wind, very few trout rising, and even fewer taking an interest in our dry flies. I tried a parcel of flies from grasshopper imitations to the ever-faithful Brown Wulff, with no luck.

Shortly before dark, Josh cast his Hornberg about 15 feet toward shore, watched it ride on the waves for about a minute, keeping his line tight. Smash! A trout pounded his fly and he brought the rod up to set the hook, cool and calm. It was a handsome 12-inch trout and we kept it, our only fish of the night. After I continued to cast for about 20 minutes, frustrated with my own lack of action, I looked at Josh and he said, very seriously, "Dad, why don't you try my rod. I've got all the fish I want."

Boy, talk about being humbled. I thanked him, thanked God for him, and told him to keep fishing. We both had all the fish we wanted.

On the Fourth of July, the Smith family enjoyed a feast of three poached trout, two of which were contributed by the twelve-year-old. I can't remember a finer meal and it had nothing to do with the food.

A generational change in streams, trout, and fishing techniques

To a 12-year-old boy, it was wilderness, a place of fantasy, escape, high adventure. The wilderness was only a short half-mile walk from his house to the very top of High Street, into a tote road through a forest of sugar maples, huge oaks, and fir thickets, over the hill and into the next valley.

He'd seen bobcat, deer, partridge, and lots of squirrels there, but it was along the small brook that meandered through the forested valley that he spent most of his time. That cold sheltered brook held wild trout, many trout, colorful trout, huge 6- and 7-inch trout. He dreamed of them often.

But the reality was even better than his dreams. Nestled in his backpack along with peanut butter and jelly sandwiches and candy bars, the boy carried a can of worms, usually dug from his 4-H award-winning garden out back of the house. Sometimes the can was brimming with huge night crawlers gently pulled from their holes on the front lawn during an evening rainstorm when his parents allowed the boy to stay up late in order to replenish his crawler supply.

Sneaking across the lawn with a flashlight, quick reaction and fast hands were required to grab the crawlers, only partly out of their holes, and gentle hands to coax them all the way out of the ground without ripping them apart. The boy was an expert. Sometimes he did so well on a rainy night that he could sell his surplus to other fishermen, friends of his dad. They used the crawlers to catch perch in Maranacook Lake.

He never told them about the trout in the brook up over the hill. Even then, he had an innate sense that too many fishermen could spoil a good thing. But he did take his buddies along sometimes and they'd make a daylong adventure out of it.

His fishing gear was basic stuff. The boy had an old rod hardly longer than himself and a small spinning reel, something his dad had discarded. A plain bare hook was tied onto the end of strong monofilament line, line hefty enough that he never lost a hook to bottom. Ever. Which was a good thing because he had only a couple of hooks.

His fishing technique was simple too. Sneak along the alders, poke the rod out over the brook just above those places where he knew a trout would be hiding, dip the hook with a gob of worms into the water, let it drift past the hiding place, and when the trout darted out, give the rod a sharp yank which hooked the fish and pulled it right out of the water and onto the bank all in one motion.

The boy knew his water, every riffle, deep pool, long bank. He didn't know this was called reading the water. He just knew where those trout lived. And he got to be an exceptional trout fisherman. Returning home on late afternoons with a creel – really just an old canvas bag he'd found in the barn – full of ten 6- and 7-inch trout – well, that was the finest kind of living for a twelve-year-old boy.

He'd clean the trout after he got home and his mom would fry them up in corn meal in a huge old cast iron skillet for supper, with lots of praise for her little sportsman who could feed his family. And boy, did those trout taste great. For the rest of his life there'd be no finer meal than wild brook trout, fried.

Of course things change, even deep, cold, fast-rushing brooks, and when the boy returned to town after college to settle into the banking profession and trudged one Saturday morning up to the end of High Street, he was surprised to find that the street had been extended deep into his wilderness. Much of the forest was gone and the last half mile of the brook he had fished so many times now flowed through a housing development.

He fished the entire length of the brook that day and caught only four trout, all less than six inches long. You can't go back, even to fish.

So the boy moved on, buying a 12-foot boat to troll the lakes for brown trout that were introduced to a lot of Maine waters that could no longer grow brook trout because of diminished water quality. Some thought the trout were lost when water in the small tributaries which fed the lakes was warmed by timber harvesting and development along their banks. Those tributaries had been trout factories in the old days. The young man thought about that, content to gas up the boat and troll for hours up and down the lake.

Sometimes he'd hit the ocean for a cooler full of mackerel taken on Christmas-tree rigs six at a time as he and his dad trolled John's Bay in Pemaquid. Lots of fun. Nothing like taking six fish at a time.

He clung to his worms too, filling up buckets with white perch during their spring spawning run and taking stringers of huge bass off their spawning beds in late May and early June with those old reliable night crawlers.

Marriage and children intruded, reducing fishing time, but before he knew it, the kids were old enough to fish. He took them perch fishing. Soon they could fling a worm and bobber out there with the best of them. A feast of fried perch wasn't hard to take either. But the kids never fished on their own. "Kids these days have too many things to do," he often said.

Occasionally, he day-dreamed about that wilderness trout stream up over High Street, but that only made him sad so he stopped thinking about it.

He progressed in his profession, started his own consulting business, and soon had amassed enough savings to think about buying a camp someplace up north in the real wilderness. More and more he found himself thinking about the old brook, those colorful trout, wilderness adventures.

His son was ten years old and his daughter was seven when the perfect camp was found on Sourdnahunk Lake just outside the northwest corner of Baxter Park, a forever wild sanctuary of 46 mountains, dozens of small ponds and miles of mountain streams. And oh yes, lots of wild brook trout.

Just one problem. Almost all of the waters were fly-fishing-only. He'd read a bit about fly fishing but never tried it. But the camp was perfect, the setting sublime, and they bought it in September as the brookies began to spawn. Oh, how beautiful those fish were – and how difficult to catch.

With a borrowed fly rod and a few Royal Coachman flies, he flayed the water in great frustration. And caught just one trout all month. But it was gorgeous, 13 inches long and very tasty. One month, one fish, but he was hooked on fly fishing.

The next spring, before going to camp, he attended LL Bean's introductory fly fishing school, a three-day adventure after which he headed to Sourdnahunk with much more enthusiasm – and an improved casting motion – and of course with a lot more gear. The new 8-weight rod and a world class collection of flies also helped. He caught a few fish, enough to feed the family a supper of fried trout several times in May and June. Yummy.

His boy began joining him at times, spending his time practicing casting with an old fly rod which his grampy purchased at a yard sale and left at camp. Even Grampy was trying this new fly fishing thing. But what really caught his attention was the daughter, casting from shore using an alder branch and string that her brother rigged up for her. She was amazing to watch. She really had the motion and rhythm down pat. Her little arm made a compact cast which was stunning in its simplicity and effectiveness.

One afternoon he took the kids to a nearby trout stream where worms were allowed and they limited out. But something didn't feel right. The trout were tiny, barely legal at six inches. Didn't fish that size used to thrill him, he wondered?

So the next time they tried the trout stream, they took the fly rods and did just as well. And because they'd eaten their fill of trout by that time, they released every single trout. It felt kind of good. As they trudged down the stream on their way out, a deer stepped into the water about 50 feet away and began drinking. When they got back to camp there were plenty of stories to tell. The empty creel didn't seem all that important.

And finally one evening as they enjoyed a stunning sunset while casting to rising trout on the lake, his son finally hit a ring and caught a trout, an eleven-inch beauty, his very first fish with a fly rod. Keeping his rod tip high he handled it like a pro bringing it quickly to the side of the boat. But when the father reached out to lift the fish into the boat, he heard his son say, "Dad, we don't need that one. Can we let it go?"

The boy's first big trout on a fly rod. And he wanted to let it go. The father couldn't believe it and tried briefly to talk his son into keeping the fish, but the boy persisted. Lifting the fish gently from the water, the father twisted the fly out of the trout's mouth, and gently released it back into the water.

After that the father started to admire the boy's casts. Somehow, quite suddenly, the boy was hitting every ring. And the father was busy releasing trout, almost too busy to fish himself. The next time the father did manage to catch a fish, he heard the boy say again, "Dad, we don't need that one. Let it go."

Oh, it was hard. Catch-and-release was not his heritage. Trout in the creel was how he judged his success. It just didn't seem right to let a keeper go. But for the boy's sake, the father began releasing fish that evening. Eventually, with both his son and daughter releasing nearly all their fish, the father caught the spirit. Now they measured their success by how many fish they released. Two or three suppers a summer of fried trout were sufficient. The rest went back into the lake.

He started thinking about that boyhood stream and all the fish he'd taken out of it. Could he have ruined it, before the developers ever arrived?

When his daughter was nine she could cast a beautiful line, so he bought her a 7 ½-foot 4-weight rod (OK, so he planned to use it himself too on some of those small alder-choked streams). The boy was twelve and tying flies by then and had become nearly a fanatic about fly fishing. He'd gotten a nice 8 ½-foot 7-weight rod for Christmas.

But the father could still outfish the boy most of the time. Then one evening, when he had taken the boat out alone for the last half hour of fishing after the sun had set, to catch one fish for his morning's breakfast, it happened.

The biggest trout of the evening was just 10 inches long, a bit disappointing in a lake that held lots of 13- and 14-inch fish. But he kept it and returned to camp. Stepping onto the camp's porch, he heard the boy exclaim, "Dad, wait til you see my fish!"

Leading the father to the cooler on the porch, the boy shined his flashlight on a monstrous trout, a 16-inch beauty, the largest ever caught by our family here at camp. The boy had cast from shore shortly after sunset and landed the huge trout.

"Gee, Dad, what's that puny fish you've got in your hand there?" laughed the boy. He ignored the barb. Looking longingly at his boy's trout he replied, "Son, that is a fantastic fish." It was the only fish the boy kept all summer.

So it was that a twelve-year-old boy fishing a stream near home with worms and filling his creel nearly every time with 6-inch brook trout, turned into a different twelve-year-old boy casting flies to eager wild brookies on a northern pond and keeping only a single fish all summer long.

50th birthday river rescue

Fiftieth birthday one day. Rescued from the Kennebec River the next. It was that kind of week.

Achieving the half-century mark, one would expect to contemplate life's meaning. Have I accomplished enough, been all that I can be, to justify five decades on this planet? A family dinner celebration at an Augusta restaurant demonstrated what is important in life and I built on that with a fishing expedition the next afternoon on the Kennebec River.

As rescues go, it wasn't all that daring — but the turnout and response from the Augusta Fire Department was impressive, if terribly embarrassing.

Stripers were few and far between, so I motored the boat up to the Edwards Dam a couple of times, up and down river, looking for those tell-tale splashes that signal active stripers. The tide was very high and a lot of water was coming down the river with a current so strong my anchor wouldn't hold.

Then the gas tank ran dry. Floating freely and fast down river, I quickly switched to the other full tank, but the motor wouldn't start. Panicked, I gave it a lot of gas – too much as it turned out. Speeding past the railroad bridge, nearly colliding with an abutment and cursing the fact I'd left my paddle at home, I pulled and pulled and pulled the starter cord. Nothing.

Finally, after sweeping under the old downtown bridge, the anchor took hold, pulling me to a stop right in the middle of the river, about even with the boat launch where this adventure had started. I caught my breath, tried the motor again unsuccessfully, and looked wistfully toward shore. There wasn't a single boat on the river but surely someone would come along who could tow me to shore.

Grabbing a rod, I decided to make the most of my dilemma and started fishing. Periodically I'd try the motor again, but no luck. No luck fishing either. After an hour, with no boats in sight, a young fellow on shore in the Water Street parking lot shouted out, "Do you need help?"

After thinking about it a minute, I decided I was ready to go home and could indeed use a tow. I knew the fire department had a boat and thought perhaps they might be willing to help me out. "Yes, I need a tow to shore," I shouted back. About two minutes later, sirens and alarms went off all over the city. "Oh God, please don't let that be for me," I prayed.

Too late for prayer. The troops were coming. If all of Water Street was on fire, I doubt there'd be a bigger response. Up and down the hillsides of the city on both sides of the river, sirens wailed. A fire truck pulled into the riverside boat launch, then an ambulance, then another ambulance, and more fire trucks than I could count.

One fireman ran to shore and began scanning the river. Sheepishly, I tried to ignore him. Then it occurred to me that they must think someone was in real trouble on the river. Using hand signals, I conveyed my need of a tow to shore. With a short wave, acknowledging his understanding, the fireman pulled out his walkie-talkie and called in the boat crew. But no one left. Indeed,

146

a crowd had gathered by now, pulled in by the sirens and excitement of a river rescue.

Gosh, was I embarrassed. As the rescue boat pulled alongside, one wide-grinning fireman inquired, "How's the fishing?"

"Not good," I replied. For a brief moment, I fantasized that no one would recognize me. But as I stepped onto the dock, fireman Dan Guimond, whom I know well, greeted me with a "Hi George!"

"Dan," I said, "today I'm Harry Vanderweide, if you don't mind."

"Well, Harry's boat does look like yours," he kindly replied.

Later, with the boat on Maranacook Lake's calmer waters, I got the gas working through and the motor purring. But I haven't shown my face on the river since the rescue. I have spent some time contemplating the future and looking into the past, considering how fortunate we are to have firemen and rescue squads, ready to respond promptly when needed.

There's a lot of rescuing that needs to be done these days. I'm starting to feel disoriented in a world that's changing so fast. Last Tuesday's Kennebec Journal reported that this November, only 150,000 resident hunters will join me for Maine's fabled deer hunt.

That's 75,000 fewer than hunted Maine's woods in 1981. It's also the smallest percentage of the state's population with big game hunting licenses, just 15.8%, since I was born. Some days I feel like I'm at anchor in the middle of a swift river, life moving quickly past, unable to get my motor going. But please, no more rescues.

Why not the best for Maine's brook trout?

With a stunning sunset to the west and a ring of pink clouds surrounding the magnificent Mount Katahdin and its surrounding mountains to the east, I had to put down my fly rod for a moment and enjoy the views. For the past 90 minutes, my view had been focused almost entirely on the yarn fly at the end of my line.

You know how it is when the brook trout are biting. A hatch of the famous Green Drakes was bringing up the trout, and plenty of them were mistaking my yarn fly for the real thing. I had already hauled in more than a dozen, and despite the intensity of my focus, missed a lot of strikes.

Nesowadnehunk (pronounced Sour-dna-hunk) is the largest fly-fishing-only lake in Maine. It isn't stocked and is chock full of native brookies. The requirement that a water be limited to fly fishing is still controversial in Maine. I don't know why that is, except that many anglers hate change. We settle into our fishing methods and cling to them like they are the Holy Grail.

I didn't get serious about fly fishing until we bought our camp on Sourdnahunk in 1991. I began with a three-day course at LL Bean where I learned to cast. That's really the critical element of fly fishing. And anyone can learn. Daughter Hilary was seven. Dad was 70.

As I sat there in the boat, enjoying the end of a blessed night of fishing, I wondered why it is that we are engaged in such a fierce battle over the management and protection of our remaining wild and native brook trout waters. After taking steps to protect just nine more wild trout waters, by banning the use of live fish as bait there, Maine's Department of Inland Fisheries and Wildlife suffered a setback last month when the legislature overturned those rules on four of those waters, to please ice fishermen.

The uproar over the rules reminded me of the fight to protect brook trout in waters that have never been stocked. As the executive director of the Sportsman's Alliance of Maine, which took the lead in that effort, I can tell you that it was not an easy path. It's a long story. Eventually, with the support of Governor Angus King and the Maine legislature, we established the "A list" of brook trout waters (waters that have never been stocked) and banned the use of live fish as bait on those waters (to prevent the inadvertent establishment of other species of fish), and the stocking of other fish.

Chandler Woodcock, now DIF&W's Commissioner, was the state senator who sponsored SAM's bill, and his hard work had a lot to do with the bill's success. No one should doubt Chandler's commitment to our wild and native brookies.

The battle has now moved to a new field – a "B list" of waters that hold wild brook trout and have not been stocked in 25 years or more. Despite the success of our protection and management of the "A list" waters, many anglers simply cannot accept the same management and protection of the "B list" waters – primarily because it would force them to change the way they fish those waters.

For 150 years, we've erred on the side of anglers – stocking every water we could reach, removing huge stringers of huge fish until there were no more huge fish, illegally establishing competing fish species like northern pike and crappie, and playing God with Maine's beautiful native brook trout. Sadly, those brook trout have disappeared from most of southern Maine and more than a thousand lakes and ponds – replaced by hatchery-reared trout and/or nonnative fish. God would have done better without our help.

As I cast a glance back toward Katahdin that night, I thought about how much I enjoy fishing for native trout in Baxter Park's small ponds, streams, and brooks. The park includes 55 lakes and ponds and hundreds of miles of brooks and streams. For more than 50 years, the native brook trout in those waters have been protected. Most of the waters are fly-fishing only. None allow the use of live fish as bait. All remain unstocked. These fish are a national treasure. And I don't think I've ever heard a word of complaint about the way they are protected and managed in the park.

So why do we not respect and protect our native and wild brook trout outside the park as well as we do inside the park? Surprisingly, even some of DIF&W's fisheries biologists – past and present – oppose protective regulations like no-live-fish-as-bait for our wild trout waters. Their opposition was an embarrassment and serious problem for Commissioner Woodcock as he sought to ban the use of live fish as bait on that very modest list of nine waters this year.

As I motored in to camp that night, so pleased by a spectacular evening of fishing for a spectacular native Maine fish in a spectacular setting, I was more convinced than ever that it is time to err on the side of the fish. You just can't deny 150 years of history, or the gorgeous national treasures at the end of my fly line that evening. They are worth protecting, fiercely, everywhere they still exist.

Blue fishing like you've never experienced it!

Rooting around in some old stories I wrote about deer hunting years ago, I discovered this October 1988 story I wrote for The Maine Sportsman. *There's a version of this story in Chris Potholm's wonderful book, "Tall Tales from the Tall Pines," published in September by Down East Books. You may think Chris' amazing tall tale about a blue fishing experience is fictional, but it's mostly truth. Here's how I told it.*

He was sitting in the hot tub when his wife Sandy reported, "Bluefish are in the bay in front of the house."

Grabbing a towel, Chris Potholm of Harpswell dashed outside. Sandy's sighting was confirmed by the thousands of poagies jamming the shore frantically trying to avoid the big blues. Chris rushed to gather up his fishing pole and launch his boat which is moored right in front of their home on a beautiful peninsula in Harpswell Sound.

Minutes later, still wearing only his towel, he was into the blues. It was early evening and he would have the fishing experience of a lifetime as the sun set and darkness settled over the sound.

He would also lose a lifetime's worth of fishing lures. With sixty-pound test on his heavy casting rod, wire leader, and surface plugs, Chris drifted as he cast to the blues. They were in a feeding frenzy. Playing each one for all it was worth, Chris had lines snapped off in his hands, lures ripped and torn from the leader, every sort of assault that a powerful fish like the blue can make. He loved every minute of it!

150

Finally, exhausted, with heavy blues up to fifteen pounds each covering the bottom of his boat, down to hand lining because that was all the equipment he had left, towel wet and soggy, body chilled by the cold damp evening air, so dark he couldn't see the fish until he got them boatside, Chris knew he'd have to head for home.

It was my very good fortune that, after finishing his time in the hot tub later that night, Chris called to invite me down to try my own luck the next day.

A bucket of blues

The inventory was complete: new surface plugs and rapalas, lots of wire leader, lead core line and fifty-pound monofilament, trolling rod and reel, cooler with ice. As each came out of the trunk enroute to Chris' boat, I couldn't have been more excited. The hot sunny day was perfect, it was two hours yet to high tide, and Chris was certain the blues were still in the Sound.

We motored into a small cove about ten minutes from his house as I rigged up my line. I thought we were going to troll and only brought my trolling rod, mistake number one. A casting rod was what was needed.

I watched as Chris cut the engine, setting us adrift. His first cast had just hit the water about thirty yards in front of the boat when a gigantic blue exploded from the depths and thrashed that lure for all it was worth. What a sight! Chris expertly landed the blue before I had even gotten a lure overboard.

After some extensive practice casts with my trolling rig, I was able to get the lure out about twenty yards, and on this day that would be plenty far enough.

BANG! My lure shot out of the water with a big blue attached! I had played him for several minutes when he exploded straight out of the water, shook himself violently, and returned to the deep, leaving my lure floating on the surface. I stood there stunned, almost out of breath. Wow!

For every blue landed, we probably lost at least two others. Twice they busted my lead core line and took expensive lures with them. One blue shattered Chris' rod right in his hands, just above the reel. I saw that rod splinter into two dozen pieces, simply amazing. And he still landed that fish!

We fished hard for three hours before the high tide slowed them down. And we had blues on nearly all the time. Sometimes several blues would return to the boat swimming beside the one which was hooked. A couple of blues were particularly memorable.

Unforgettable blue

An inept cast had left my surface lure just ten yards off the stern and I angrily reeled it in. As I began to lift the lure off the water right in front of me, the ocean parted and a massive blue lunged for it.

POW! Water cascaded all over me as the blue returned to the water with my lure firmly in his mouth. He'd risen from directly under the boat. I was startled but recovered in time to play that blue for five minutes until he snapped my line.

Two casts later, out about twenty yards this time, a new surface lure was hit and I began a long but losing battle with another blue. He took the line out another twenty yards and then suddenly blasted up and out of the water, dancing about fifteen feet across the Sound until the lure was shaken loose. I'll never forget the sight of that blue dancing across the top of the water.

When action slowed at high tide, my cooler was full of eleven blues ranging from six to fifteen pounds. Most were at least ten pounds. I had cleaned them as they were caught and put them immediately on ice. We chummed with the remains. The last four blues were left out for photos back at the house and cleaned afterwards.

As we returned to the dock, Chris' boat looked like a war zone. My shoulder ached and my feet were wet and numb. I thanked and acknowledged Chris as a superb guide. It had been a day of dreams, hefty fish smashing surface lures, battling and jumping and thrashing, giving no quarter, powerful powerful fish.

Linda broiled some filets for dinner that night, with a little butter and lemon, about three minutes on each side. I never had a better tasting fish, and the freezer is now full of them. Bon appetit, Chris!

Reflections on Maine fishing

They follow state hatchery trucks, eager to catch those fat brook trout stocked this month all over the state. They crowd roadsides, casting from bridges. They troll the shores of lakes and ponds, hoping to catch a landlocked salmon.

Some seek a feed of tasty perch; others dream of a huge northern pike. Many focus on bass, Maine's most popular fish. Twice as many bass are caught every year than brook trout. An angler army is out this week on the brooks, streams, rivers, ponds, and lakes. But the troops are depleted and we're losing our recreational fishing economy.

Maine falls far short of its potential when it comes to inland and coastal recreational fishing. We lack investment, management, infrastructure including water access, and marketing.

Between 1995 and 2003, we lost 30,000 nonresident anglers, a 28 percent loss, representing an economic hit of $20 million or more. Sales of fishing licenses to nonresidents peaked in 1989 at 108,698. But this problem is not limited to nonresidents. Mainers have given up fishing here as well. Sales of fishing licenses to residents peaked in 1991 at 203,245. Total fishing license sales peaked in 1990 at 310,278. Last year we were down more than 50,000 licenses since that peak year.

Ironically, to address our current budget problems, the Governor proposed that the Department of Inland Fisheries and Wildlife eliminate its only marketing position, stop attending out-of-state sportsmen's shows, postpone publications of important fishing brochures and other information, and, unbelievably, stop

153

providing fishing rule books. The legislature's Fish and Wildlife and Appropriations Committees have reversed some of those decisions.

Recreational fishing currently contributes significantly to our economy. The 2006 National Survey of Fishing, Hunting, and Wildlife-Associated Recreation reported that $257,124,000 was spent in Maine by anglers. Nonresidents spent $124,812,000. This includes both fresh and saltwater angling. But we could be doing so much better. The federal survey reported 10,000 more nonresidents fished freshwater in New Hampshire than Maine in 2006! And 25,000 more nonresidents fished in Montana than Maine.

With more investment, better management, and strong marketing, recreational fishing can deliver a lot more to our economy. This matters to many Mainers, from the two guys at Kennebec Lures who make fishing lures in their Sanford garage, to the locally owned fly shop, to the retired warden who ties and sells flies in the north country, to the guides and sporting camps all over the state.

Let's examine one part of this equation: stocked fish. In 2008, DIF&W stocked 1.3 million fish totaling 360,000 pounds. In 1996, Colorado's Division of Wildlife stocked more than 65 million warm water fish and 14.6 million cold-water fish, including 4.8 million catchable-sized rainbow trout. Guess where people go to fish these days?

A Hatchery Commission was established in 1999 to assess and evaluate Maine's recreational fish production facilities and set production goals at state-owned facilities. The Hatchery Commission recommended fish production goals of 1,958,063 fish weighing 865,077 pounds by 2012. In 2008 we fell 658,000 fish and 505,000 pounds short of our goal. And 2012 is fast approaching.

Then there is the problem of access. Maine is blessed with a lot of public water, about a million acres in nearly 2,000 lakes and ponds, 32,000 miles of rivers, brooks and streams, and over 3,000 miles of coastline. While the state ranks only 39th among states in land area, it ranks 9th in total water area, not counting small water

154

bodies. It places 4th in miles of tidal shoreline, 4th in lake acreage, and 11th in river miles.

The value of this resource goes well beyond these statistics: few states have water resources of the quality found in Maine. I've often said that Maine's rivers are the arteries in our economic body.

Yet our legal access to this abundance of water is very limited. There are hundreds of lakes and ponds without any legal public access, and the places where we do have access are not always well known.

And Mainers have no legal access to moving water. We have walk-in access rights to Great Ponds, and that's it. We have no legal access to brooks, streams, and rivers. Adjacent landowners own the land under our rivers, brooks, and streams and can prevent us from even standing in those waters. The Maine legislature has addressed some of these problems and the Sportsman's Alliance of Maine and other groups are working together to improve fishing in our state. You can help. Go fish.

Of brookies and bass and grandsons

The 14-inch wild native brook trout took the first dry fly offered when I arrived at my favorite pool about a mile from the road in this cold, free-flowing north woods stream. The trout's stunning spawning colors erased any doubt that there is a God.

In the last 10 years, Maine has stepped up protection of its native brookies, important when you understand that this state has 97 percent of all the remaining native brook trout lake and pond habitat in the United States.

Wading downstream to my favorite pool holding hundreds of spawning trout (I caught more than 50 in two hours), I'd been forced out of the stream at one point when three large river otters took a disliking to my presence. They were more aggressive than the cow moose and calf I'd walked around at the point I entered the stream.

Not long before I'd driven to camp to enjoy this fall fishing experience, I'd taken my grandson to a favorite pond near my Mount Vernon home, just 20 miles from the state capitol, to fish for smallmouth bass. Six-year-old Addison sat in the front seat of the old aluminum canoe and cast a jig toward shore, working it back as skillfully as a professional bass angler, while his grandfather watched with a mixture of love, pride, and anticipation.

There! An eager bass grabbed the jig, Addi lifted the rod, the fish was on, the fish was up and out of the water! "That's a huge fish, Addison!" I exclaimed. And his smile told me that the public purchase of land surrounding this pond in the Kennebec Highlands was a very wise decision.

Maine added two million acres in the last decade to its public lands inventory to make sure all of us have access to this state's amazing natural resources. As a river angler, I've been blessed to fish magnificent rivers from Alaska to Montana to Quebec and Labrador. Maine's rivers are equally spectacular.

In July, I slipped my kayak into the Kennebec River just 15 miles north of the capitol city of Augusta. The 47 smallmouth bass caught that morning were memorable, as were the two dozen Bald Eagles along the river. Most astonishing – I didn't see another person! And this section of the river is so undeveloped you'd think you were in the Alaskan bush.

Waters all over the state draw my attention year-round, yet I remain true to my roots. Nothing pleases me more than a day on a small brook, catching brook trout. My first fishing experiences involved dunking worms into tiny brooks. Today I prefer to cast flies.

My favorite brook regularly gives up as many as 100 brookies in a half-day of fishing. Except for that day I waded a mile down the brook and got mixed up with a pair of mating bears. That called for a hasty retreat! No need to retreat if you're thinking of fishing here.

Salty fishing

I've always enjoyed fishing the salt water, and we've got a lot of it in Maine – more than 3500 miles of coastline, plus magnificent rivers. Mackerel have been a lifelong entertainment, and I remember trolling for them outside of Rockland harbor with my dad. One time a shark grabbed my mackerel – something I have not forgotten! Dad and I also fished off Pemaquid, launching the boat at the landing behind the old fort, and trolling outside the harbor. We always filled a cooler with mackerel.

For a while, bluefish were plentiful along the coast, and both Dad and I loved to catch them. They are powerful fish that jump out of and dance over the surface of the ocean, quite a scene. Then the striped bass arrived, and they became an obsession. Dad and I liked to fish the lower Kennebec River with our friend Harry Vanderweide.

Dad and I were well known for our old (OK, very old) fishing gear, and the first time Harry took us, both our reels froze up after one striper was caught. I remember hauling my fish in by hand, after the reel failed. Fortunately, Harry always had a lot of fishing gear in the boat. We'd watch for a flock of gulls, hovering over the water, and motor over, because that's where the stripers would be. It was great fun.

One day we'd hauled in so many fish that Harry got lazy on the final fish of the day, setting aside the gaff to haul in the striper by hand. In the process, two hooks on the lure buried deep in his hand. The fish was still hooked, and Harry turned to me to help him out. I grabbed the fish first, as it flopped around, causing Harry great pain and anguish, and after a bit of a struggle, I got the fish unhooked.

Then Harry handed me a set of pliers and told me to rip the hooks out of his hand. I looked at him in disbelief. But he was serious and insistent. I nearly lost my breakfast, but I ripped the hooks out. Blood poured out too, and Harry looked like he was going to faint, but he wrapped his hand in a towel and motored to shore, where we sat for a while. And then we got back in the boat, motored up river to Bath, loaded the boat on the trailer, and Harry drove us home, his hand still wrapped in that bloody towel.

Before they removed the Edwards Dam in Augusta, it was a superb place to catch stripers coming up river. I used to go over there on my lunch hour from the SAM office and fish, generally catching 10 or 12 big stripers. One time, I reeled in the lure to my side, and just as I lifted it from the water, a big striper leaped out of the water and grabbed the lure – no more than 3 feet from my side. A royal battle ensued, and I eventually got him back to my side and released him.

Lubec

We spend time every summer way Downeast in Lubec where my mom grew up. Mackerel fishing has always been superb there, and I've enjoyed catching them from the dock in Lubec and another dock over on Campobello Island.

One summer, while fishing from the Lubec dock, I had a strike and knew right off it was not a mackerel. The fish nearly yanked the rod out of my hands, and took off out into the bay. The fight went on for about 15 minutes, and a crowd gathered round. When I finally got the fish to the dock, I was surprised to find that it was an Atlantic salmon.

There are salmon pens within sight of the dock, so I wondered if this was a wild fish or one that had escaped from a pen. And I wasn't sure of the rules and didn't know if I could keep the fish or not. Everyone in the crowd assured me it was okay and urged me to keep the fish. Then the Harbor Master wandered down from his cove side office, having noticed the gathered crowd, and he also told me it was legal to keep the fish. So I did.

I took it back to our campsite at Cobscook State Park and grilled it that night, sharing it with other family members and folks who were camping nearby.

When we got home, I stopped in to the Augusta headquarters of the Department of Inland Fisheries and Wildlife and asked Peter

Bourque, the Fisheries Division Director at the time, if it was legal to keep an Atlantic salmon if you caught it off the dock in Lubec. Peter said it was not legal. And that's when my story became a hypothetical one!

Penned salmon

I did eventually find a way to keep an Atlantic salmon. The feds had ordered an aquaculture company to get rid of all of its salmon, because they were too close, genetically, to wild salmon, and if they got out of the pen, could mess with the wild fish. Originally the company announced it would kill and bury the fish, and that's when I got involved.

I took lots of anglers to Machiasport, where we boated out to the pens, stood on the sides of them, and caught the fish, which went up to 35 pounds. I can't even describe the excitement when you saw a huge salmon coming up from the depths, headed for your lure. Some of my fly fishing elitist friends were appalled – until I took them with me one day, and they caught the salmon on flies. After that, they begged to return!

Later, the company allowed anglers, for a fee, to catch and keep the salmon, and several groups did that, many coming from out of state. But that was a short-lived opportunity and eventually the rest of the salmon went to the Indian tribes. Thankfully, none were wasted, and every time I returned with a cooler full of salmon filets, I shared them with neighbors – making me very popular in the neighborhood for a while!

Fishing, hunting, and birding the world

Yes, I've been lucky

Speaking to a class of students at the University of Maine at Machias, all of whom hoped for fish and wildlife careers, I was asked how I managed to create a career that required me to hunt and fish. Yes, I've been lucky!

I've been lucky in my friends, my job, and my opportunities to travel. My first two trips to Alaska were with my friend Les Priest, who had a travel business focused on lodges in that great state. I accompanied Les to Alaska to visit the lodges he represented, and you'll read of some of our amazing adventures. At a national convention of sporting groups and businesses, I met the manager of a lodge in a remote section of Alaska. He ended up inviting my wife Linda and me to his lodge, where we starred in a new video for him and I wrote stories for his new website. My story, "Loving Alaska with Linda", tells you all about this wonderful experience.

My friend Harry Vanderweide, who cohosted the TV talk show *Wildfire* with me for 13 years, also had his own TV show, *Northeast Outdoors*, and invited me along on several trips to tape *Northeast Outdoors* shows. In the Florida Keys, I caught 23 species of fish in three days. Phenomenal! Our adventures at Lake Mistassini and the Rupert River, as well as at Lake Watshishou, were special too. But the best place Harry ever took me was the Leaf River in far northern Quebec. It's the best place to catch wild brook trout in the world. I've enjoyed three trips there, all of them unforgettable.

Maine native and friend of mine Joe Sowerby, owner of Montana Fly Fishing Connection and the best guide I've ever fished with, invited me to float the Smith River with him, and after that, every time I managed to get to Montana for a conference, I spent a few extra days there exploring other Montana rivers with Joe.

After Linda and I became avid birders, friends who lived in a nearby town invited us to spend a week in the get-away house they'd built on the west coast of Costa Rica. What a trip! And that led us to birding adventures throughout Texas and Arizona. We've even enjoyed birding in Italy – those Hoopoe's are amazing birds!

In 2015 I started posting photo essays of some of these trips on my website, www.georgesmithmaine.com, if you'd like to see them. Just flick back through my outdoor news blog.

Alaska is the real wilderness

Alaska is what Maine wants to be, or perhaps what Maine used to be. Real roadless wilderness. Abundant natural resources. Free-flowing rivers teeming with fish. Less than 250,000 people in 586,000 square miles (compared to Maine's 33,000 square miles), and another 250,000 in Anchorage, a city ringed by majestic mountains sitting on the shore of breathtakingly beautiful Cook Inlet. A people characterized by rugged independence and individualism.

I have returned from two weeks in Alaska with Les Priest of Readfield, owner of Alaska Outdoor Adventures. Less is booking agent for numerous Alaskan lodges and outfitters and took me along for the adventure of a lifetime while he checked out new client lodges.

Les specializes in smaller lodges which provide exceptional service and fantastic fishing, and outfitters who provide an unbelievable level of comfort even on the most adventurous rafting and wilderness trips. We visited five clients and stayed in everything from tents to luxurious lodges. We fished morning, noon and night.

The sun doesn't set until 10:30 p.m. and some days we used all available light before turning in our fishing rods for a few hours of sleep, then rising at 5:00 a.m. to get out on the water again. I've never experienced such incredible fishing.

We began by fishing the famous Russian and Kenai Rivers where millions of sockeye salmon were spawning. These fish enter the rivers fresh, sporting a silver color, then turn bright red with a

161

green face as they get ready to spawn. Males grow large humps and are particularly menacing looking. We caught all three varieties, fresh sockeye, reds, and humpies, fishing with the exceptional guides of Osprey Alaska.

Then we jumped into a plane for the interior, arriving at the 300-mile-long Iliamna Lake where I was delighted to find lodge proprietor Len Batchelder to be a Maine native.

Fishing the Newhalen River with rafting guide Rich Rothley of Dream Creek Outfitters, we caught Dollie Varden trout, grayling, and sockeyes. Rich gave us a real thrill by piloting the boat to within 20 yards of a sizeable grizzly bear wandering the shoreline, stopping every once in a while to jump into the river for a fish, and giving us very sharp glances. We were close enough to see him licking his lips, and I wasn't sure whether that was for the fish or for us.

Then it was on to the Copper River Lodge, where Dennis and Sharon McCracken's rustic log home guards the mouth of what must be the most spectacular rainbow trout river in the country. Tossing flies to huge bows in a river so clear that we could see them piled up behind the spawning sockeyes, would be an incredible thrill for any fly fisherman. Landing a rainbow over two feet long, as I did, was simply an indescribable breathtaking experience. The river is all catch-and-release fishing – showing what Maine could have if we were as bold as Alaskans in protecting our strongest sport fishery.

Traveling through Alaska on float planes with Willow Air Service provided a sense of the immensity of the wilderness, the rivers, the mountains, and the tundra. Next, we flew into Hidden, Alaska, a lodge over 100 miles from any road, where we traveled for two hours on four wheelers through a gorgeous untouched mountain meadow and hiked a game trail for a third hour to reach a secret creek which, as far as we know, had never been fished. Now that is spectacular! When Les pulled two trophy-sized grayling and a handsome rainbow from one pool in just the few minutes we had, we both knew this was a creek we had to get back to.

The proprietors of Hidden Alaska, Sharon and Buck Bowden, homesteaded a splendid lodge located on Skeeter Lake where I caught and released 41 greyling in an hour of fishing with a dry fly, after which I returned to the lodge for a hot steamy sauna followed by a wonderful meal of halibut. Even in the Alaska bush, you eat well.

Les and I hiked trails where wolf and bear tracks predominated, and marveled at Sharon and Buck's cabin, covered by the teeth and claw marks left by visiting black and brown bears. This is wilderness!

We finished our trip with a visit to Angel Haven Lodge, sitting on a bluff with Mt. McKinley at your back, and the huge Yentna River at your doorstep. We covered over a hundred miles of the river each day with Tom and Larry Angel, fishing tributaries that were teeming with silver salmon, another species known for their spectacular aerial display.

Les has a video of one of my salmon coming out of the water three times to dance across a 30-yard-wide creek, and finishing with a double-flip somersault. Wow! Alaskan memories, the finest kind.

The glory that is Alaska

"The character of place defines us," wrote John Haines, poet laureate of Alaska. "Place makes people."

Maine is my place. But after a recent trip to Alaska, I think this could have been my place, in different circumstances. Maine and Alaska share many characteristics. Fierce independence. Parochialism. Quiet confidence. Modesty. A wry sense of humor. An understanding that our lives are governed by seasons and the weather – but that there is no weather that can keep us inside.

Alaska is Maine writ large. Everything there is bigger. Moose grow to 1800 pounds, compared to our smaller beasts which top out at about 1400 pounds. Even Alaska's largest city, Anchorage, is much bigger than ours, Portland.

In Alaska there is more of everything. More mountains. More trees. More fish (definitely more fish). More snow (usually). More rain. More raw energy. There is also less. Less people (only 250,00 outside of Anchorage, spread around 586,000 square miles). Less regulation – a lot less. Less turmoil. Less reason to go elsewhere.

Alaskans ask each other, "Have you ever been out?" They mean out of Alaska. Many have not. It isn't easy to get here from there. I met Mainers all over Alaska, even in the remotest wilderness. And they looked to be right at home. Most did not miss Maine.

Perhaps because we did hit so many remote lodges, I ran into a lot of homesteaders – people who have carved their homes out of wilderness sites, who thrive in the challenges of wilderness living, who delight in their dependence on the land and its bounty. Alaskans are entitled to one moose and five caribou per year, for subsistence.

Even though most do not take advantage of this bounty, it seems to define their place in the world. They believe in using their natural resources and fish and wildlife for their own purposes. Indeed, it's difficult (and expensive) to live in Alaska and not use these abundant resources. Most use them wisely. But their sense of the Alaskan environment is that it is there to serve them.

There's a sense of wildness even in downtown Anchorage, where guns, sporting goods and taxidermists are plentiful. In the elegant Regal Hotel, the lobby is full of stuffed wildlife: an impressive 1500-pound polar bear, a 10-foot brown bear, moose, sheep, goat, and musk ox.

Imagine a major downtown Portland hotel lobby stuffed with mounts of Maine bear, moose, deer, bobcat, and more. Unimaginable really, because we have lost touch with subsistence wilderness living and because most Mainers do not hunt and are unfamiliar with firearms.

Alaskans were about to vote in their party primaries and I saw candidates in newspaper and even television ads toting firearms. One candidate's road signs said, "Vote for me. Catch more fish." In Maine this year we entertained 18 gubernatorial candidates, only one of whom hunts. And she didn't advertise that fact. No candidate dares appear on TV with a firearm.

Alaskans have a real sense of adventure, possibly because the sun shines nearly 24 hours a day in the summer. But that is offset by total darkness during part of the winter. That causes a lot of hopelessness, depression, and alcoholism.

Those who survive and thrive in Alaska tend to be smart, creative, bold, happy with themselves, self-reliant, and able to take whatever comes their way from grizzlies to 20 feet of snow. Several of our Alaskan guides were well-educated. One had a master's degree in wildlife biology. Another had just received a master's in English. Both wanted to be writers. Each had a well-defined sense of place in Alaska. Neither was an Alaskan native.

I think we Mainers tend to think of ourselves in an Alaskan situation, but that is a false sense of place. We don't live in the wilderness. Indeed, there is no wilderness in Maine, no roadless areas of mountains, forests, and rivers. We don't hunt for subsistence. We certainly don't carry guns on the street or in TV ads. Many Mainers are afraid of guns.

But we are not far removed from Alaska, either. Alaskans have more guns per capita than any other state. But Maine is second. Alaskans revere their environment, while getting the most out of it. We love our northern forests, but harvest them for jobs and income.

Both Mainers and Alaskans are defined by the character of their states. In Alaska, it is a definition driven by wilderness, great rivers, a huge coastline, magnificent wildlife, awesome mountains, a tough climate, and a dependence on natural resources for sustenance and a living.

Forced to fish Kodiak Island's Karluk River for five more days

Kodiac Island, Alaska, is a sportsman's dream. Years ago, when I got stranded there for five days at the mouth of the Karluk River earlier, some people didn't believe me. Stranded in Alaska? Right!

Traveling with Les Priest of Readfield, who organized the trip through a company he owned at that time, Alaska Outdoors Adventures, we enjoyed a five-day adventurous raft trip down the Karluk River with outfitter Fishing Alaska Style, owned by Maine native Jeff Pyska who lived in Alaska.

Our guide for the week was Augusta, Maine, resident Bob Smith, who did a superb job of putting us onto lots of King Salmon and keeping the river's huge brown bears out of our tent camps.

Alaskan summer days linger late. The sun shines bright up until 11:00 p.m. and it never gets totally dark. On the third day of our trip I fished for 16 hours, finally stepping out of the water at 1:00 a.m. so Bob, who stood guard on the riverbank to make sure bears did not bother me, could get some rest.

About 10:00 p.m. a large brown bear emerged from the alders directly behind me. Bob shouted, "Bear!" That got my attention right away and I quickly abandoned the river, stumbling up the shore to the protection of camp and Bob's rifle.

That bear was driven off by Bob's shouting but I fished closer to camp for the rest of the night, glancing nervously over my shoulder on each cast. My last salmon of the night was huge and took line 200 yards down river, but I did not follow, breaking him off, worried about the bear.

About midnight, in the dusky twilight, preparing to cast, I glanced directly behind me to a small inlet brook where a couple of harvested King Salmon lay in the shallow water, kept for tomorrow's dinner. A nose poked out of the tall grass. I whirled around, fearing a close encounter with a bear when a fox emerged. Whew! I chased him away from the salmon and kept casting.

The next morning I emerged from the tent to sit on the boxed-in-toilet that Bob had set out back in the alders. Finishing my business there, I turned around to gaze into the alders as I pulled up my pants, and there, strolling by no more than 25 yards away, was a massive brown bear. If he'd walked by in front of me while I was seated on the toilet, I wouldn't have needed to go to the bathroom for a week!

Kodiak Island is a gorgeous combination of lush hills, high snowcapped mountains, boiling rivers and the sea, about the size of Connecticut and, as Les noted, "a weather pattern that nobody can figure out."

At the end of our fabulous wilderness adventure we were stuck for five days at the mouth of the Karluk River, waiting for the fog to lift so a float plane could pick us up. The problem was complicated by the fact that the plane could land only on a high tide.

Bob kept our spirits up. Camp cook Jeff Madore kept us well fed. And we just kept on fishing. It helped that a run of Sockeye Salmon passed right in front of our campsite each day.

After two days of waiting patiently for a plane, we moved up the bay to a small native Indian village for hot showers and real beds. Out of the tents at last, clean and comfortable, with stunning scenery and a bay full of salmon, I might never have left if my family didn't draw me back to Maine. I called wife Linda every night from the village, letting her know I was still stranded there. Not sure she ever believed me!

After landing over 50 King Salmon, hooking and losing many more in ferocious battles, seeing brown bear every day, being accompanied everywhere by flocks of Bald Eagles, and enjoying a true wilderness experience, I yearn to return.

Just before we broke camp and moved into the Indian village, Les and I were 500 yards from camp fishing the bay, and standing in the water quite a ways off shore, when we heard, in unison, the remaining eight members of our party yell, "Bear!" Between us and camp a huge brown bear sauntered down over the hill and stood on the shore, Les and I on one side, camp – guides – and safety on the other.

Bob and Assistant Guide Pete Potter rushed down the shore with guns, hoping to chase the bear back up the hill rather than toward Les and me. I stood mesmerized in the water, prepared to chuck the rod and swim into the bay if the bear approached. Not a great strategy. Luckily the bear retreated up the hill, leaving us with nothing but another fine memory and putting an exclamation mark on our wilderness adventure.

The day before we finally packed up, Bob, Les, and I boated back to the mouth of the river where Sockeye Salmon were migrating through. Standing in a slough of fast water, fishing with fly rods and large red and green salmon flies, we caught dozens of salmon. On light rods, these 10- to 15-pound fish were all we could handle. I'll bet a thousand Sockeyes passed me that afternoon.

As we motored back to the Indian village, knowing that we were already four days overdue at home, I couldn't help but secretly wish for one more day of fishing. But my good luck on the Karluk was over. The float plane picked us up the next morning.

Loving Alaska with Linda

I fell in love with Kamishak and my wife was there to see it. Kami wasn't my only new love that week – just the first. Little Ku stole my heart one day, the more full-bodied Moraine another. But I kept coming back to Kami and made her my final choice.

On a week-long vacation at Rainbow River Lodge in Iliamna, Alaska, our first look at Kami was from high above her in a float plane. She's a big coastal river, but not distinguishable from other Alaskan beauties from the air. However, once we started up river in a boat and spotted a huge brown bear on the first gravel bar, the Kami's special allure grabbed me.

By the time our guide beached the boat at our first fishing location, we'd seen – up close – ten brown bears including a sow with two cubs – and I'd used up my first roll of film. If you're fishing the Kami, bring lots of film.

In three days there, we saw 17, 20, and 25 bears respectively – and we did respect them. They fished beside us like longtime angling buddies, wrestled each other, frolicked in the river, and generally ignored us. It was hard to ignore them. Even harder to ignore were the fish. Huge Coho Salmon, called silvers, stacked like logs in calm pools, resting on their way up the rapid river to spawning grounds. Colorful Dolly Varden trout lay in every riffle of fast water, feeding on salmon eggs.

I was particularly delighted to find we could catch silvers on the surface, using a large fly that we dragged across the top of the water – sort of like fishing for bass. This worked each morning for a short while, and then we'd switch to subsurface flies – still using floating line on our 8-weight rods.

And guess what: the fly of choice was a green clouser – the same fly I employ for trout in Maine! You'd drift the clouser just under the surface, draw it past the silver of choice – because almost all of this is sight fishing – and hold your breath when the fish turned to gulp the fly. Often these fish would follow the fly a distance, sometimes waiting to take it almost at your feet. Wow!

Linda and I battled hefty 11- and 12-pound silvers all morning that first day with Kami, then switched to Dollies to rest our aching shoulders, getting – no exaggeration – a fish on every other cast with many over 20 inches. My biggest Dolly was a six-pound brute.

For Dollies we used five-weight rods and a bead that resembled a pink or red salmon egg. It was important to get the color of the bead right, just one of many reasons that the employment of a guide makes a lot of sense. Eager to take our flies and tough fighters, the green-tinted Dollies are too often ignored in these world-renowned salmon and rainbow trout waters. But we loved their eagerness and their fight and we took every opportunity to fish for them.

Of course, we'd traveled all the way from Maine to this first-class Alaskan wilderness lodge to catch giant rainbow trout – so our love affair with the Kamishak and her bears and silvers and Dollies was an unexpected surprise. The rainbows did not disappoint. Many exceeded 20 inches in length and either of the two 27-inch eight-pound fish I caught – one on the intriguing Little Ku (Nanuktuk River), the other from the bigger Moraine Creek – would have been the thrill of a lifetime for any avid angler.

For three days on the rainbow rivers, we used light five-weight fly rods, stood surrounded by spawning red and pink salmon amidst stunning scenery in cold rushing rivers, peered into the water to see gigantic rainbows lying in wait, drifted our flies past the selected fish, watched as the fish grabbed our fly, set the hook, and took a deep breath – so we could yell: "Fish On!"

A relative novice with a fly rod, experienced only with small Maine brook trout, with one trip to Quebec where she caught some big landlocked salmon, Linda was somewhat stressed, worried that she would not cast well enough or be able to land these big Alaskan brutes.

But with good advice from our guides she had no problem at all, learned a great deal, experienced more catching of big fish in a week than you'd get in a lifetime of fly fishing in Maine, and landed as many of her fish as even the most experienced anglers that week (including yours truly, who had a hard time learning that you can't just horse these fish in).

Traveling to other states and countries is always interesting. Traveling to Alaska is so much more – exciting, inspiring, with jaw-dropping beauty, massive mountain chains harboring glistening glaciers, high country tundra, a stunning coastline, rivers, lakes and ponds of all sizes, all on a scale that is unimaginable to anyone in the lower forty.

And did I mention the bears? I am amazed by the photos of Lin calmly casting her fly while a huge bear – sporting a light brown coat – stood nearby watching her. She went from a state of terror about the bears to complete nonchalance. Well, honestly, she was wary but not worried.

Rainbow River Lodge managers Chad and Nicole Hewitt might have missed the first Alaskan gold rush, but today, there's still plenty of gold in the fishery found in this state's coastal and inland waters, thanks to savvy fisheries management, good research, and an understanding of what spectacular fishing can do for a state's economy and people. No rainbow trout in this entire area can be killed. It's all catch-and-release angling for trout with barbless hooks. Three salmon per day may be kept and the lodge staff filets, freezes and packs them for you.

Lin and I also rode the train from Anchorage to Denali National Park, where Mt. McKinley peaked at us through the smoke generated from fires that have burned more than five million acres in Alaska this year. In this stunning national park, we saw lots of caribou, mountain sheep, grizzlies, and three of the biggest bull moose you'd ever see – Alaskan moose are about a third larger than Maine's.

But it's Rainbow River Lodge and the fishing that I will never forget. This was the best fishing I have ever enjoyed in my life. The lodge offers my kind of wilderness experience: gorgeous comfortable cabins, hot showers, gourmet food, superb service, super friendly staff, gracious hosts – all in a family environment where baby Hewitt joined us every evening for dinner.

This is a fly-out lodge, where – every day – you are able to fly to your selected river to fish for your favorite species. Admittedly, this is pampered angling – until the first big rainbow or silver is on your line and you've got to go to work. Both rainbows and silvers take to the air as soon as you set the hook, and you sometimes think your heart will burst before, finally, you find the fish at your feet, ready to be released.

The variety of angling experiences available here are impressive. A couple of anglers from California wanted a day of dry fly fishing – hard to find in August – but Chad flew them to the headwater of the Copper River, where they hiked the upper river catching lots of rainbows and grayling – an extraordinarily beautiful fish that flies out of the water, often taking your fly as it returns to the surface.

Another group flew to the Iliamna River and proclaimed it the most beautiful setting in which they had ever fished – with lots of rainbows to boot. This group said the Iliamna was their favorite of all the rivers they fished that week – hard for me to imagine after experiencing the Moraine, Ku, Gibraltar, and Kamishak.

But then, one group chose to raft and fish the Gibraltar on their final day and reported it was the best rainbow fishing they'd had – another surprise because I liked the Moraine and the Ku the best for rainbows.

One evening, Eric Wolf from Connecticut and I lugged a canoe over a nearby beaver dam to fish one of the "Pike Lakes" in back of the lodge. You can guess what species awaits eager anglers in these waters. Catching large northern pike on eight-weight rods, popping mice on the surface of this wilderness pond, we were excited beyond description. We fished until it was pitch black, and then turned to discover we didn't know where we'd started this adventure. The entire shoreline looked the same!

Eventually, we found the beaver dam and returned safely to the lodge, arriving about midnight. Of course, it remains light until after 11:00 p.m., giving relentless anglers more fishing opportunity after dinner. This was the only night I fished after dinner – every other evening we were exhausted by the day's angling in these mighty rivers.

So here will be your dilemma in this angler's paradise: with so many species, so many big fish, and so many amazing rivers, when Chad asks, as he does after dinner every evening, where you want to fish the next day, what will you say? Believe me, that's the most stress you'll feel all week.

Home only a month, I already yearn to return to Alaska and Rainbow River Lodge. I will never forget my love affair with Kami, Little Ku, and Moraine.

Lunker trout at Labrador's Little Minipi

Harvey and Betty Calden are veteran sporting camp owners who offer the very best in hospitality and outdoor experiences, focused on hunting and fishing. Tim Pond Camps in Eustis, Maine, was always Betty's project while Harvey focused on their camps in northern Quebec and Labrador. In August of 1999 I took my son Josh, when he was 16, to Harvey's Little Minipi Camp in Labrador and we had a phenomenal experience, catching over 50 brook trout over five pounds – topped by Josh's seven-pound brookie and 7 ½-pound Arctic Char.

The views of Little Minipi Lake from the lodge and the home pool, only a five-minute walk – were great, but a short boat ride across the lake put us on the river. And Josh kept all the guests well supplied with flies – wooly buggers and mice worked best. We fished about a mile of the river, enjoying a variety of weather, and caught big fish every day. We lost as many fish as we landed, had many more rises and strikes, and were into heavy fish constantly.

We also caught some "small" trout – two and three pounds! Fishing the "Honey Hole" was a favorite, about a half mile down the left side of the river, where we caught most of our char. My last two fish from this pool were brookies that took me right into the backing on my reel. I landed a six-pound trout here that spit out a fly our guide had lost over a month before when his client broke off the fish.

One of the lodge's guests, Marty Faley of New Jersey, was stunned with a brookie over ten pounds – on his first day of fishing here. The 26-inch beauty had a girth of 17 inches. But just because all fish are released, you should not think that you can't have a beautiful mount. In fact, Marty commissioned a wooden carving of his 10-pound trout from Maine's own Gene Bahr, one of the finest wildlife carvers and artists in the nation. Gene has fished the Little Minipi himself and can duplicate the colors of your fish precisely. Give him a few photos and measurements, and you'll have a trophy for the wall that will last through many generations. Your family will still be talking about your fish a hundred years from now!

Although brook trout were our targets, we caught a few Arctic Char – just starting their spawning run up the river – and northern pike which put on a real acrobatic show and strong fight. Josh took top honors with the seven and one-half pound char while I landed a 10-pound pike. We hit the Triple Crown – trout, char, and pike – on two different days. Our Newfoundland guide, Marvin, was very protective of the fish, and made sure every fish was released alive and well, after slipping out the barbless hook.

On Thursday, Josh put on a show at the Boulder Pool, keeping me running for the camera as he pulled in fish after fish. Josh's excellent casting ability was impressive to all the anglers in camp, and allowed him to reach pools none of the rest of us could cast to. Finally, after a couple of hours, Josh took a break so I could fish!

Our last day was a rainy deluge, but Josh and I persevered to enjoy the finest day a father and son could ever hope for: five trout each, all over five pounds. At the Honey Hole, my last two fish were six and six and one-half pounds, and Josh's last fish was a six-pound beauty that rose to his mouse. I caught all of mine on a wooly bugger, flies that Josh had tied the night before.

Motoring across the lake on our final trip back to the lodge, we looked back to see a full rainbow spanning the lake – a magnificent end to a spectacular trip, a lifetime memory for both of us.

Brook trout heaven – Quebec's Leaf River

As an old brook trout fisherman, I can only hope heaven is as good as this place. When death darkens my door, perhaps my eyes will suddenly open on the Leaf River, with an eternity of fishing ahead. Hallelujah! The fishing at this northern Quebec River is as good as it gets, with brook and lake trout plus the bonus of an occasional Atlantic salmon.

Because I'm an outdoor writer, associated with a TV production company and a travel agency, and executive director of Maine's largest sportsmen's organization, I've been blessed with many free trips to Alaska, Montana, Quebec and Labrador. In fact, I'd been to the Leaf in 2005 on a free trip to produce TV shows with Harry Vanderweide, host of *Northeast Journal*.

Normally I don't return to a place, because there are always new places available, for free. In fact, I've never paid for a fishing trip out of state before. But this year, I returned to the Leaf – and I paid for the trip. That's how much I love this river.

If trout fishing was an Olympic event, the Leaf River is where you'd hold it. This big river in the northern tundra is a world-class venue. Let me tell you about one morning when we fished "the funnel," perhaps my favorite place on the river.

Our excellent and experienced guide, Serge, put us ashore about 200 yards below this spot where the river narrows sharply, a mountain of water rushing through and over huge boulders, quiet deep pools of fish along the shore. I hiked to the top of the funnel, passing a complete set of caribou antlers, weathered on the shore right where the animal had dropped them.

The Leaf gives you a lot more than fish. Migrating caribou trot across the tundra, then swim the river – often right where you are fishing. One morning we saw a beautiful silver wolf – swimming across a very wide place in the river. We boated up to him for photos. What a thrill! Musk ox and even black bears are sometimes seen beside this river.

But of course, it's the fishing that brought me back and this particular morning at the top of the funnel will tell you why. A ripple of water flowed about five feet from shore and I casually cast a muddler in brook trout colors. Pow! A huge trout burst through the surface and grabbed the fly. The fight was on, and he took me well into the backing as my 5-weight rod had all the fish it could handle.

When the trout was finally at my feet, I lifted it with my boga grip to check the weight: a hefty 3 ½ pounds. It is no exaggeration to say the next seven casts caught seven trout between 1 ½ and 3 ½ pounds. They all rose to take the muddler on the surface.

Stepping up river about 20 yards to check out the quiet pool at the top of this run, I gasped. Huge trout lay all over the pool. Switching to a dry fly, a large Royal Wulf, I was astonished to see, as soon as it settled on the water, three gigantic trout rise to fight over it.

That pool produced 50 trout for me in about two hours of heavenly angling – none smaller than 1 ½ pounds. Many were 2 ½ to 3 ½ pounds. One was more memorable than the others. He looked big when he splashed to the surface to gobble my fly, and he took me down river in the rapids very quickly, breaking my tippet and stealing my Royal Wulf – the only one in my fly box.

Forced to try other flies, I found a few that attracted these trout – but none as successful as the Royal Wulf. About a half hour later, another huge trout rose to take a large Stimulator, and he too headed quickly into the rapids. But this time I skipped along the shore and kept up with him. After a ten-minute battle, he was at my feet – the biggest trout I'd seen in this river – and I carefully photographed him lying in the water, then used the boga grip to check his weight: four pounds!

While his weight and girth were surprising, the biggest surprise came when I grabbed the fly to remove it from his jaw. As my fingers reached for the fly, I stared at it in confusion. I was looking at my Royal Wulf – not the stimulator I'd cast! It was the Royal Wulf that I'd lost about a half hour earlier! On one side of his jaw was my Royal Wulf, and on the other side, the Stimulator. This was the same fish I'd broken off earlier.

I reattached the Wulf to my line and got back to catching trout on every cast.

One other fish in that pool was memorable. A large lake trout could be seen in the pool – and it chased the trout on my line quite often, sometimes grabbing my trout and fighting for them. Finally, I tied on a large green bass fly and tossed it into the current. On the first drift the laker grabbed it, and the fight was on. I landed him about ten minutes later. He weighed six pounds.

Although the Leaf is famous for its brookies – what they call "speckles" – the river also offers the challenge of lake trout – a tough, strong fish that will give you all the fight you can stand. One day I broke off four big lakers. If you catch a smallish trout – two pounds on this river – oftentimes a laker will grab it and fight you for it.

I won't soon forget one of these lakers. He chased a small trout up to my feet, grabbed it before I could, and took off across the river, as I struggled to stop him. About 150 yards out, he actually broke my line. He wasn't hooked. He just wouldn't let go of that brookie. After landing six lakers from six to seven pounds, and breaking off four larger lakers, I can tell you that some of your most remarkable fish will be lake trout.

Yes, there are salmon

I've never been an Atlantic salmon angler – too many casts required to catch too few fish. Too many fishless weeks. But the Leaf River holds salmon and occasionally we'd spent time in specific pools trying to catch one.

We began my last day on the river in just such a pool – actually several pools alongside a short but ferocious run of rapids. I'd picked up only a few brook trout in the upper pools and got to the final pool at the tail end of the rapids with vastly lowered expectations.

When I felt a tug on the line and picked it up, I knew I had a big fish, and I was thinking lake trout when the salmon leaped high out of the water. I shouted and my fishing partner across the river, Herb Morse, says I was jumping up and down. I don't remember. Too excited.

After a 20-minute fight and six breathtaking leaps, the 8-pound fresh-from-the-sea bright silver salmon lay where I'd placed him in shallow quiet water near shore. For ten minutes, I sat with him, as happy as an angler could hope to be, until he swam away to continue his journey home.

Now, I'm an Atlantic salmon angler.

A walk along the river

I love to hike a river, searching for fish, and the Leaf offers the best hiking I've ever experienced. It's those isolated unnoticed unfished pools that can surprise you with memorable fish.

On a cold blustery morning, I'd already hiked a caribou trail along the river for about two miles, fishing small pocket water and catching some real nice trout, when I gazed down at what I thought looked like an ideal pool: a ripple of water flowing over a cluster of large boulders, water about four feet deep.

I snuck down over the bank, took a position behind a large boulder, and carefully cast a muddler about ten feet out. As it settled to the surface, there was a vicious splash as a large brookie grabbed it. He took me into my backing three times, and when finally brought to shore, he topped three pounds, a fish of beautiful colors.

I set him in quiet water to get his strength back, checked my fly and line, and cast to the same spot. Bam! Another big one. As I brought this trout into the quiet water, trout #1 pulled out. This is how it went for about a half hour.

When the guide called me to a delicious shore lunch (fish, of course), I'd hauled seven huge brook trout out of that small boulder-strewn pool, all larger than two pounds including one four-pound bruiser. One had taken my fly deep into his mouth so he got to keep it – I cut if off rather than risk killing the trout to remove the fly.

After lunch in a quiet cove with a beautiful sandy beach, where we spotted fresh wolf tracks, I hustled back to the same pool. My dry fly caught one more three-pound trout. Then I switched to a heavy bass fly to catch two more very memorable fish – another four-pound brookie, and the tenth and final fish, a big surprise, a six-pound lake trout.

One pool, ten fish, two to six pounds, a lifetime memory, discovered on my morning walk along the Leaf River.

What I like about the Leaf River

Experienced guides, large brook trout, strong lake trout, magnificent Atlantic salmon, a big noisy river, walks along the shore searching for pools of trout, migrating caribou, a wolf swimming the river, lots of hearty food for breakfast and dinner, delicious shore lunches of potatoes and trout, jet boats skimming over huge submerged boulders, barren rocky tundra as far as you can see, northern lights, comfortable cabins, hot showers, flush toilets, but most of all – the fish and the river that holds them.

Loving Lake Watshishou

Mainers are often reluctant travelers. Many have not even traversed the entire state in which they live. My folks had never been to Baxter State Park in northern Maine until Linda and I purchased a camp near there. Few Mainers have been to Acadia National Park, even though every year it is one of the most visited national parks in the nation.

Aroostook County is unknown to most Mainers, its rolling hills full of potatoes and other crops unseen. And I have talked with folks from northern Maine who have never been south of Bangor. My grandmother Searles lived almost all of her long life in Lubec, staring across ten miles of water to Grand Manan Island – and she never set foot on it.

Canada might as well be in the Far East to most of us. My first visit to Montreal, only four hours away, came just last year at the age of 52. Last week, I paid my first visit to the city of Quebec, just five hours from my house. I can report that it is a good thing to visit these places. Linda and I loved both Montreal and Quebec City.

But what really captivated us last week was the north shore of the St. Lawrence Seaway, featuring hundreds of miles of stunning scenery, expansive beaches, mountainous terrain, amazing waterfalls, rivers teeming with fish, and small well-kept villages nestled alongside every harbor. To describe it in current lingo, it's life the way it should be.

We traveled to Quebec to fish, but the trip along the St. Lawrence up to Havre St. Pierre, our jumping off place for the wilderness fishing adventure, added a truly spectacular element to our trip that was unexpected. It's worth the drive, on Route 173.

Seven hundred and fifty miles later, after 13 ½ hours of driving, we entered the small coastal village of Havre St. Pierre, where we would catch a float plane to Lake Watshishou, home base of Lac Holt Outfitters and our hosts Gilles Marquis and Lisette Bouchard.

We were there to fish, but the wonderful hospitality offered by Gilles and Lisette, the gourmet food, the very comfortable lodge, the view up the lake – well, it was all very special. Inveterate reader that I am, you will know that this must have been a very special place when I tell you I took six books with me and managed to read only 20 pages the entire week!

Day one found us in Pool 55 at the mouth of the Watshishou River at 6:00 a.m., where a 3 ½-pound landlocked salmon struck my fly in the first hour of fishing. Few fish battle as strongly as landlocked salmon, or jump as high. This fish did not disappoint, and it took about 10 minutes to bring it to hand. After a quick photo, it was released unharmed. Both Linda and Edye Cronk, our traveling companion, also caught several nice fish that morning.

Let me describe my experience this way. I caught 36 landlocked salmon and 24 brook trout. My salmon were 3/12, 4/14, and 5 pounds, and a giant of 27 inches that weighed six pounds. And that was the first day! It was a day I shall never forget.

But it will be the last day that stays freshest in my mind. An aggressive salmon in my favorite pool on the river had, on two previous days, tried to steal a smaller salmon off our lines. I was determined to catch this big salmon, and tried many flies and approaches, without luck.

Linda and I returned to that pool for our last morning of fishing, and she caught many nice salmon and trout up to about a pound and a half. As the last hour of fishing arrived, I decided to implement my plan for the big salmon. Using two split shot weights and a large Black Ghost fly, I snuck up behind the ledge at the bend in the pool and dropped the line into a deep hole on the other side of the ledge where I thought the huge salmon might be hiding.

As the fly settled to the bottom of the hole, something strong picked it up. I knew immediately that I had hooked the big salmon. Linda says my fist pumped up and down, but I have no recollection of that. The salmon slowly took about a hundred yards of my line out into the river, and when I finally pulled back, he ripped another hundred yards down river and leaped magnificently out of the water. We both gasped.

"I did it. I got the big salmon!" I yelled.

It was a tremendous fight, with many heart-stopping jumps, and I was shaking when he finally arrived at my hand, where I measured and weighed him – a solid 27 inches and 5 pounds. After photos, he was released to fight another day and thrill another angler. I took my rod apart, finished for the day and the trip - and very, very happy.

Montana's Smith River

Joe Sowerby stood in thigh-deep water, coaching me to bring a colorful Smith River brown trout to his net. Perched in the front seat of a raft, I marveled at the fight in this trout, hooked when Joe directed my cast into the fast water only inches deep along a grassy bank.

Finally I got the fish between Joe and me. "Bring him up to me," he instructed patiently. "Lift that rod tip straight up." When I did, that brownie leaped four feet into the air. Joe leaped too, about three feet to his right and caught the 18-inch fish mid-air in his net!

"Wow! What a catch," I exclaimed, as my fishing partner Dave Sowerby and I hooted and hollered. I'd never seen that before – a mid-air catch into the net.

Something else I'd never seen was Montana's famous Smith River Canyon, where we enjoyed a spectacular 5-day float and fish trip with pink and yellow 1000-foot high limestone cliffs surrounding us like a protective cocoon. This is a very special place.

And the fish? Well, they are special – and plentiful, too.

Joe owns Montana Flyfishing Connection, a team of superb guides who could lead even a novice fly fisher to quality brown and rainbow trout in this awesome river canyon. We also caught whitefish and a few grayling.

Along for this June 2003 adventure were Edye Cronk, President of the Sportsman's Alliance of Maine, Joe's dad David Sowerby, his Uncle Doyle Sowerby, and Doyle's daughter Debbie. We are all Maine residents – and we've made Joe, a Maine native, our Montana connection. If you prefer other Montana rivers and trips, Joe offers a variety of angling adventures – but I strongly recommend the five-day Smith River float – a powerful package of scenery and fish.

The rafts are sturdy with one guide for every two anglers. The tents and cots are comfortable and the camp sites stunningly beautiful with fishable water right in front of your tent perched on the riverbank. There's something about the sound of moving water that makes me sleep better at night.

Each morning the crew breaks camps and moves everything down river where it is all set up again when you arrive at the new campsite after a day of rafting and fishing. The food is remarkable too – the best I've ever enjoyed on a trip of this type. Most restaurants don't serve food this good – and I'm serious.

Hors d'oeuvres of shrimp cocktail and fried nuggets of goose. Asparagus, fresh fruit, unbelievably tasty marinated pork with chutney sauce, mouth-watering grilled salmon, garlic-mashed potatoes – even pecan pie! And quality wine with dinner. All transported for five days in coolers in the rafts.

Wildlife is abundant in the canyon – especially birds. We saw Golden and Bald Eagles, Peregrine falcons, mule deer, whitetail deer, lots of antelope, and hundreds of geese with their goslings. From great blue herons to Kingfishers – they're all here.

Picture this. Our dinner table is laid out on the river bank. I sit facing the river about 20 feet away, as I cut into one of the most delicious pieces of pork I've ever enjoyed. A fresh salad, garlic bread, mashed potatoes, and a fine Merlot portend a splendid dining experience after a fabulous day of rafting and fishing.

Facing me is a beautiful limestone wall on the other side of the river. I spot an osprey perched in a softwood tree on top of the cliff. Just as I'm pointing out the bird to my companions, the osprey dives straight into the water, with a big splash, and emerges with a fish. Now that's entertainment!

I was particularly surprised that – in mid-June – there were no bugs. I never once put on bug spray.

One evening, Dave and I, guided by Joe, lingered long on the river, arriving late for dinner, to enjoy some evening dry fly fishing. In a couple hours I landed 12 trout, including 18- and 19-inch browns. Dave caught an equal number including a monstrous 21-inch brown trout.

We fished from the raft and also got out to wade some of the best sections. Although the days were hot, we managed to catch fish consistently – even though I have often said that brown trout are the most challenging and difficult fish to catch.

My favorite fishing time came every morning between 5:30 a.m. and 6:00 a.m., when I wandered up and down the river on my own, wading and casting. Those solitary peaceful mornings always produced memorable rainbows and browns. And I enjoyed watching the sunlight work its way down the canyon walls.

When I returned to camp, bacon would be sizzling and the coffee would be hot and plentiful. Did I tell you about the food yet? If you take this trip, insist on a spicy breakfast burrito some morning – but use the hot sauce sparingly – or have plenty of Tums!

As you can imagine with a company called the Montana Flyfishing Connection, this was strictly fly fishing – both subsurface and surface depending on the conditions and time of day. The size of the flies surprised me. They are huge – nothing like the tiny flies we use in Maine to catch trout. My five-weight rod was satisfactory although it would have been easier to cast some of those big diving sculpin and floating golden stoneflies with a heavier rod. And the bugmeister fly – well, it was so effective it ought to be illegal!

But my proudest moment came when I caught three rainbows and two browns one morning before breakfast right in front of our campsite with a fly purchased in Rangeley – the CDC emerger.

One brownie was so big that Dave had to wade out with a net for me.

Although I've been fly fishing for 12 years, I learned a lot from Joe and his experienced guides. I'll be a much better antler after this trip with them.

My second proudest moment came the last day with Joe guiding Dave and me again. I'd been steadily improving my technique in getting those flies into holes under the limestone walls and big river boulders. Joe pointed out a boulder up ahead on the left as the raft approached, and encouraged me to try to put my fly right into the indentation with a small pocket of water in the middle of the boulder. And I did!

The take was immediate, with a big splash, and a 17-inch brown trout was on. They needed a wide-angle lens to photograph my grin as I brought the trout to the net.

Four casts – four fish

As our raft glided by, Doyle Sowerby stood casting toward the cliff into a small side channel of water. We were gazing at the "birthing cave" high above us on the sheer cliff wall until Doyle's shouts got our attention.

He gestured wildly and shouted, "Four casts, four fish, 18 inches!" We thought he was kidding.

But we should have known better. Guided by his nephew Joe, Doyle had stepped out of his raft, cast what he described as four of the best casts of his life right into the undercurrent bank of that cliff, and pulled out four brown trout, all 18 inches long.

I accused him of pulling out the same trout four times. But no brown trout gives you more than a single chance. What a thrill!

Sitting in the river

After a very hot and sunny day on the river, I arrived at our campsite exhausted. When I mentioned a swim, Steve, a member of the crew, pointed out a small boulder about mid-river.

"You can sit in a small hole in the river with your back up against that boulder," he suggested. Stashing my rod and back pack near my riverside tent, I grabbed a beer and waded out to the rock.

"Ahhh," was all I could muster for comment as I settled into the cold river. Very refreshing. And the boulder was just perfect as a back rest.

I'd been sitting there about 20 minutes when Dave Sowerby's raft arrived, and he joined me, replenishing my cold beverage. We were sitting there in the river, recounting a splendid day of fishing, when our outfitter, Joe Sowerby, waded out with hot appetizers of fried nuggets of goose for us. Now that's service!

Conservation is king in Costa Rica

The tiny Central American country of Costa Rica could teach Maine a few things. Two million tourists a year drive the Costa Rican economy that employs half the working population. Their environment is their economy. Where have we heard that before?

In April of 2011 Linda and I visited Costa Rica for the first time, staying at the vacation home that Bruce and Peggy Bornstein of Wayne, Maine, built high above the Pacific Ocean in Nosara. The Bornsteins' heavenly perch is called Casa de Suenos, House of Dreams. They share their dream with friends and also rent it out when they're not there. Our visit to Casa de Suenos was our Viaje de Suenos, Trip of Dreams.

Nosara is a remote area on the Nicoya Peninsula. The last 30 kilometers to get there are over atrocious gravel roads. We drove through a river that had no bridge and rarely got beyond third gear in our five-gear 4-wheel drive vehicle. It was a real adventure!

Costa Rica comprises only .01 percent of the earth's landmass, but harbors 5% of the earth's biodiversity, including more than

10,000 identified plant species, 9,000 butterflies and moths, and 500 species of mammal, reptiles, and amphibians. For avid birders like Linda and me, the astonishing 880 species of birds in this country that's the size of West Virginia was what brought us here.

Google these birds and prepare to be astonished: Elegant and Violacaeous Trogons, Turquoise-browed Motmot, Long-tailed Manakin, White-fronted Parrot, Squirrel Cuckoo, Great Kiskadee, Rufous-naped Wren, Orange-chinned Parakeet, and Canivet's Emerald. The names alone are exciting. Wait til you see the birds!

In the past decade, Costa Rica has taken strong steps to protect its rich biodiversity. More than 11 percent of the country is protected in a national park system and another 10% to 15% in private and public reserves. But we saw all of our birds around the Bornsteins' house, at the beach, or in the city of Liberia. We also saw variegated squirrels, coati, a Black Ctenosaw (think giant lizard), and entire families of Howler Monkeys. They surrounded our house and entertained us for hours.

Costa Rica offers lots of activities for tourists from zip lines to world-class fishing. But you should never go there without a bird book and binoculars. When I was looking for advice about birding in Costa Rica, I turned to Maine's top birding guide, Bob Duchesne, a state legislator and the author of the *Maine Birding Guide*.

"Costa Rica is UNBELIEVABLE!" exclaimed Bob. "It has as many birds as all of North America. I've never seen anything like it. Costa Rica is one of the reasons I got interested in nature-based tourism in Maine. I said to myself, if Costa Rica can do it, why can't we?" Indeed.

North Dakota pheasants – wild and fast!

The sky was full of pheasants, barreling right at me at what seemed to be 100 miles an hour. Up went the shotgun. I fired once. Twice. I reloaded. Fired again. Fired again. And I missed them all!

Pheasant hunting in Regent, North Dakota is humbling. The four misses happened on the second day of our four-day hunt. Well, it was raining and my glasses were fogged up. And the pheasants are fast. The gray sky made it difficult to distinguish the roosters from the hens as they flew at me, and you can only shoot roosters. And I'm not very good on passing shots. Those are all the excuses I could come up with.

On the third day, in the very same spot along the lake, a big rooster (the male pheasant) rose in front of Nellie, our dog, and flew by me at supersonic speed. And I killed it! My best shot of the week. Pheasant hunting in North Dakota is fantastic!

These are wild, tough, wary pheasants, not the pheasants raised in Maine by fish and game clubs and put out in the fall to be hunted. And the pheasant population here is huge. Last year hunters shot a half-million pheasants and that was a down year!

So you might think it would be easy to shoot your daily limit of three birds. You would be wrong. These birds generally lift off 100 yards or more in front of you. It's uncanny. Even when they're in deep grass, they know you're coming.

This was my sixth year of pheasant hunting here, an annual trip I look forward to all year, taken with hunting friends from Maine and other states. On this trip Bill Martens, Larry Pauling, and Ken Bear from Pennsylvania joined three Mainers, Paul Edmonds, Kal Kotkas, and me.

We ate well, thanks to Kal's exceptional cooking skills. We hunted well, thanks to Larry's dog Nellie. The thick grass and tangled weeds make it very difficult to find a downed bird – particularly if it's still mobile. A good dog is essential, not so much for pointing the birds but for retrieving the birds.

There's a lot of strategy involved. Some hunters walk through the corn and wheat, while others stand at the end of the rows, as much as a mile ahead. We call them blockers. They get some shooting as the birds fly ahead of the walkers. But the walkers get most of the shooting.

Many of the pheasants run ahead of the walkers and pile up at the end of the rows, unwilling to run out into the open. When the walkers get to the end of the rows, pheasants take off in all directions. It's wild!

Our outfitter, Jim Binstock, is a farmer and he puts us up in a house he owns in town (population 160). We spend most of our time hunting Jim's square-mile farm, which he maintains mostly for the pheasants. He also leases other farms to grow both commercial crops and pheasants.

The first year I participated in this hunt, North Dakota was anchored in depression. This year, thanks to the shale oil and the fracking process, the state is booming, with the lowest unemployment rate in the nation. We're two hours from the oil fields but our favorite Regent house is no longer available. It's full of oil workers. But Binstock puts us up in a very nice house, four bedrooms, eleven beds, a nice kitchen, two baths. We don't rough it.

Lessons learned

We always learn things on these trips. One member of our hunting group saved $4 by purchasing a crushed beat-up taped-up box of shotgun shells in Bismarck. Many of the shells misfired. We kidded the guy all week. He threw the shells away and bought new ones in Regent after a very frustrating first day of hunting.

I love the terrain here. Wide open plains. You can see for fifty miles. Very few trees. Nothing like Maine.

The first year I visited, I noticed that the targets at Binstock's firing range were set at 500 yards. This is the distance they typically shoot deer! I've never shot a deer over 125 yards in Maine.

Another lesson learned

Paul Edmonds shot a beautiful rooster, very colorful, light blue, golden yellow, deep reds. He carried it around for 10 minutes, then brought it over to us for a photo. He laid it at our feet and told us about how he'd found and shot it, for at least five minutes.

Then he handed me his camera and moved the bird slightly to set it up for the photo. That was when the bird raised its head and took off, running through the field with Paul in hot pursuit, with me following a short distance behind him, carrying his shotgun. I think there was quite a bit of shouting, probably mostly on my part.

I have learned in past years that you can't catch a wounded pheasant that's on the run. On one hunt, I knocked down a pheasant, walked up to him, reached down to pick him up, and he jumped up and took off running. I never saw him again. So I was pretty pessimistic that we'd catch Paul's pheasant. But Paul was determined and we lucked out when the pheasant stopped to hide about 30 yards away. I handed Paul his shotgun and he shot the bird. For the second time. This time it was dead. And we got the photo.

Hunting trips feature extraordinary cuisine. And this trip to North Dakota is special, because Kal Kotkas is a superb cook. Kal planned the menu, featuring beef stew, pea soup, fresh salads, and his fabulous pheasant stroganoff, a dish we call Pheasant a la Kal. We also had a great spaghetti dinner featuring from-scratch venison tomato sauce made by Bill Martens. Wow!

For my part, I got my three birds on day one, shooting respectably well, thanks mostly to a shooting lesson I got before I left Maine from Brad Varney in Richmond. On day two, I shot poorly, ending the day with two birds. I could have shot a third bird right at dusk. But after walking more than 10 miles that day (a typical day), I just didn't have it in me to shoot that bird.

On day three, except for one appalling miss, I shot well and made my best shot of the trip, the bird mentioned at the top of this column. Brad Varney would have been proud of me.

On our final day, we left the house at 7:00 a.m. It was still dark, 26 degrees, wind howling about 25 miles an hour. I was wearing all the hunting clothes I brought with me. In the first two corn and wheat fields we walked, I got no shots, although we put up a bunch of pheasants.

189

In the millet field along the river, I blocked while three of the guys and the dog walked up through the field. I was ducked down behind a small rise when a hen pheasant popped over the rise and nearly hit me in the head. It was flying at least 50 miles an hour, with the wind, and would have knocked me out for sure. It passed no more than three feet over my head. I was thrilled.

Just before lunch, I finally shot a bird. We took a long leisurely break at noon, warming up, enjoying a lunch of leftovers and sandwiches. At 1:30 p.m. we got back after them, and in the first two pieces, I missed a couple of birds. Then it's on to the lake, where the birds pile up in the williwags. Sure enough, on the first hunt there, I made a fantastic passing shot, dropped a pheasant, but lost it. It apparently ran off after hitting the ground.

In the next hunt, along the north side of the lake, we put up hundreds of pheasants, and I shot two, completing my daily limit. On the final pheasant of our final day of hunting, I used my final shotgun shell. Good planning!

But this trip is not about the numbers of pheasants harvested. On day two, Paul Edmunds and I sat at the end of a road, waiting to be picked up, watched a Golden Eagle soar by, enjoyed a stunningly beautiful sunset across the plains, talked about (OK bragged about) our grandchildren, and watched two pheasants walk out onto the road, not far from us. Neither of us made a move to shoot them.

Cree Nation features unforgettable fishing adventure

The explosive strike of a large northern pike startled me – even though I intensely anticipated it. The viciousness and speed of this toothy aquatic predator is astonishing. This one – a 12-pound 28-inch fish – ripped out my line, then swam swiftly toward me and made a dash right under the boat. Only some quick rod handling on my part and a sturdy steel leader kept the fish attached to the line and to me.

Imagine a small grassy cove full of 8- to 15-pound pike pounding surface lures one fish after another until we were exhausted. Actually, there is no need to imagine this because the experience is real – and no more than 15 hours by motor vehicle from Augusta. Flying gets you there even quicker.

Mistassini Lake in northern Quebec, over 100 miles long and 30 miles wide was my destination for six days of angling with Harry Vanderweide and Andy Collar of URSUS productions, to tape segments for their television show *Northeast Outdoors*.

The entire northern half of this huge lake is the exclusive territory of the Cree Nation and its outfitters. We were the guests of Osprey Lodge located on an island near the 51st parallel in a beautiful setting with new cabins constructed in the last five years. Osprey delivered solitude, exceptional food, superior service, all the modern comforts, and best of all – tons of fish. This place is an angler's dream. Depending on time of year, anglers here focus on lake trout, brook trout, walleye or pike. Lakers grow upwards of 50 pounds – we saw one that topped 30 pounds.

Osprey also offers an interesting opportunity to learn about Cree history and culture. I thoroughly enjoyed my days on the water with our Cree guides who were very willing to share information about their history and background and who also possessed superb fishing skills.

Arriving mid-morning on our first day, after spending the night in Chibougamau, we hit the lake quickly and trolled for lake trout, catching several fish. I don't usually enjoy trolling, nor am I a lake trout man, so it came as a surprise when I found myself intensely anticipating every strike and fish. Most of the camp's guests at this time of year target lake trout because they are plentiful and huge. I quickly got into trolling and thoroughly enjoyed the day.

But it was my last fish of the day – a 21-inch 3 ½ pound brook trout with beautiful lavender spots – that made the day for this old Maine wild brook trout fanatic. This gorgeous trout was seven inches longer than any trout I'd caught in Maine this year.

After a splendid breakfast on day two, we boated 50 miles north to the far end of the lake. The modern Lund boat with a 50-

horse four-stroke motor glided over a surprisingly glassy surface. We sat in a boat on a 2000 square mile mirror. A fog bank to the west obscured the shore making it impossible to tell where the water ended and the clouds began. It was one seamless shimmering surreal silver tableau.

And we were the only anglers enjoying about a thousand square miles of it on this splendid morning. This place is real wilderness – remote, quiet, stunningly beautiful. The boat stopped in a quiet cove at the north end of the lake and my first cast brought an eager walleye to hand. Harry likes to say he doesn't really like fishing – he just likes catching. He really liked this day!

In an hour and a half, I boated 25 walleye, most between one and three pounds. Then it was time for our Cree guides, Norman and Eric, to cook up a few of these tasty fish for a shore lunch. I have never enjoyed a tastier fish – no exaggeration. Walleye filets cooked over an open fire, accompanied by fried onions, potatoes, and beans, were better than any meal at the finest restaurant.

Insisting that we had enough video of walleye, Andy directed us on to northern pike. Anxious to produce the most video possible, he was a slave driver. We had to fish, fish, and fish some more. It was brutal.

Coasting along slowly, casting into the grassy shallows along the shore, we started catching pike immediately. The word frenzy would not be sufficient to describe our afternoon's fishing as huge pike pounded our lures constantly. Having caught only a few pike in my life, I was unprepared for the exciting action they provide. Pike strike viciously, fight tenaciously, and appear prehistorically fierce. I loved them. In one small cove alone we caught dozens of hefty pike on surface lures. Harry even caught one that held his lure sideways, not hooked but not willing to let go. It was truly amazing fishing.

Exhausted, with a long boat ride back to camp for dinner, we reluctantly pulled in the lures and headed back to camp. Actually, I was still casting as the boat picked up speed out of the cove. At 7:00 p.m., we entered the teepee where all of Osprey Lodge's guests are served their final dinner. We were very glad we'd returned to camp.

The large table that seats 16 guests and guides was covered with food. First course: moose and caribou stroganoff. Second course: caribou meat pie, the most delicious meat pie I've ever had, and I ate three helpings to make sure my opinion would not change.

Third course: a 16-pound lake trout caught by an angler the day before and donated for our dinner. Various salads and breads accompanied the feast, including bannock bread stuffed with the eggs of lake trout. I consumed six pieces of that, again to confirm that it was delicious. It was. Then came dessert. Or I should say desserts. Yes, I tried them all, just to be polite, from home-baked donuts to chocolate cake. Wow!

Luckily, the walk back to my camp was all downhill. On the porch, rigging rods for the next day's fishing when we were to concentrate on brook trout, I saw a fish rise in the cove. Probably a whitefish, I thought. I didn't even try to catch one of those. Probably should have. The guides were smoking whitefish and lake trout that night in an open air outdoor hot smoking structure, for guests to take home.

A few guests who fished most of the day for lake trout and then fell short of their daily limit of eight walleye were going out for evening fishing to fill their walleye quota. As they walked past, I didn't tell them I'd caught 26 walleye in less than 2 hours that morning – three times the daily limit – and returned all of them to the water.

Rupert River fishing

The morning Harry Vanderweide, Andy Collar, and I were scheduled to fly on from Osprey Lodge on Mistassini Lake to another Cree camp on the Rupert River, I convinced my young Cree guide to take me walleye fishing. We motored down the lake to a good spot where I caught dozens of fish – so many that I hated to leave. We were scheduled to fly out at noon, and we did cut it close. As we were motoring down the lake toward camp, my guide looked up and said, "George, I think that is your plane." Yes, Harry and Andy had left without me! I had to motor 50 miles across the lake to catch up with them at the Louis Jolliet Camp on the Rupert River.

When I finally arrived, Harry and Andy were sitting on the porch of one of the camps, laughing. It's always good that I can amuse and entertain them. But strangely, there was no one else there. We were sure the Cree were expecting us, so we moved into a camp, and made our own dinner in the kitchen that night. The next morning, several boatloads of Cree arrived. They had returned to their village for a funeral.

To those of us born to brook trout fishing in Maine, nothing is better than a river teeming with brookies, especially if some of them are over five pounds. Some anglers might prefer a river full of lake trout. And others might be more interested in a river of walleye. I know anglers who get really excited about a river chock full of those toothy predators, northern pike.

But imagine this: the Rupert River in northern Quebec has all four species! In numbers! In huge sizes! Before I describe this angler heaven, a confession is in order. I'm now a walleye man. And I have come to believe that real men fish for northern pike.

My July visit to Louis Jolliet Camp, owned and operated by the Cree Indian Nation, situated on a high bluff above the Rupert River, can be summed up in one anecdote. My Cree guide, a young man of 19 years named Abraham, boated up the river about 20 minutes to a small cove indistinguishable from dozens of others in this magnificent watershed. Intent on catching walleyes that morning, the best-tasting fish I've ever had, I tied on a yellow grub to my spinning line and cast it toward shore.

"Fish on!" I exclaimed. It's always good to start your fishing day with a first cast that brings in a fish. This was a medium sized walleye of about two pounds, and Abraham put him in the cooler for lunch. In the first hour, I'd boated about 15 fish when a weak strike was followed by a sharp tug on the line. A battle ensued with much line being taken out by the fish, until I finally got it to the side of the boat.

"Hey, look at that," said Abraham. "A pike has your walleye." Sure enough, the small walleye hooked on my grub was ensconced in the toothy grasp of an 8-pound pike. The pike had the walleye cross-wise in its mouth and was not about to let go of its meal. Even though the pike was not hooked, it finned beside the boat with the walleye in its mouth.

Andy and Harry, here to film TV shows for *Northeast Outdoors*, boated over to shoot some video of the pike underwater, and the fish steadfastly stayed in place beside the boat. I took a few photographs of the fish and then we decided to let the pike have his lunch. Very gently, I pulled the grub out of the walleye's mouth, and we watched the pike slowly sink beneath the surface with the walleye still firmly in its grasp. Perhaps you can see why I fell in love with northern pike. They are very aggressive!

Here at Louis Jolliet Camp to catch lake and brook trout, for which Quebec and this camp are well known, I quickly cast aside a life-long allegiance to brookies in favor of a fling with walleye and pike. Walleye I enjoyed because they are plentiful, easy to catch, and delicious cooked on the shore over an open fire. Pike I liked because of their ferocious strikes, aggression, speed and fight. I caught them with a spinning rod, under the surface with spinner baits and on the surface with banjo minnows.

After a lot of that, I took up the fly rod and caught them with a light 5-weight rod and a floating mouse. Now that was a thrill – bringing long runs and terrific battles by even the smallest pike.

Not to sell brookies short. Harry did catch a beautiful 5-pound brook trout even though we were there in early July, too soon for the best brook trout fishing that comes in August and September when the large fish move into the river to spawn. And we did enough trolling for lakers to put together a decent television show. I caught more than Harry, which made my day. He'll tell you otherwise but you know you can believe me.

This river has some beautiful water for wading but we were not there long enough for me to give that a try. We did all of our angling from boats. There also appeared to be a nice population of whitefish, but again, not enough time in just two days to angle for them.

Louis Jolliet Camp is an old sporting camp purchased in 1998 by the Cree Indian Nation of Mistassini that owns the surrounding land. The camp sits in the midst of the James Bay territory that covers 127,000 square miles, about 1/5 the area of Quebec. Huge amounts of water surround the camp that sits on a high bluff with beautiful views. Only 20,000 people reside in that huge area, including 12,000 Cree, many of whom still make their living from traditional activities: fishing, hunting, and trapping. Abraham pointed out the area where his grandfather traps beaver as we boated up river one day.

To say we were blessed with solitude and isolation at Louis Jolliet Camp would be a significant understatement. Harry, Andy and I were the only anglers on the river for the two days we fished there. All that water is reserved for the camp and its guests. Amazing! A generator keeps the camp's water system and electricity on for 24 hours a day, providing all the comforts of home.

One of the benefits of visiting this camp is the opportunity to live and learn the culture of the Cree. All of the staff at the camp is Cree and very friendly. As we dined, we could hear the girls in the kitchen who were always laughing and singing. One had a particularly beautiful voice and we lingered over coffee just to hear her singing in the kitchen. I could not understand the language, but you did not have to know the words to understand the timeless message it conveyed, in this very special place only a few hours from the hectic world we live in, but so far away, so far away. Whether it is your kitchen staff singing or your fishing line, a visit to Louis Jolliet Camp will put a smile on your face and a song in your heart.

Texas birding adventure

The state bird of Texas is the white plastic bag. Millions dot the highways, stuck to the trees and bushes. At a distance in a marsh they are often mistaken for snowy egrets. You can tell the difference quite easily in the strong Texas wind, because the bags move a lot more than the egrets.

In April of 2009, vacationing along the south Texas coast and Rio Grande Valley to watch birds, our first impression was dust and depression - a long drought drying up streams and ponds, the deepening recession closing many restaurants and small businesses. But in the Aransas National Wildlife Refuge on our first morning, with a luminescent Blue Grosbeak in our binoculars, the dust and drought were forgotten. Texas is a birder's paradise, albeit a dry one.

Look! There's a Summer Tanager! What color! Over there! An Altamira Oriole! Look at that orange! There's a Painted Bunting! All in one tree! Honestly, in two trees on Bird Trail 2 at Aransas we saw nine different species and a stunning display of color. And this was just our first day in Texas.

As the week's temperatures climbed to the mid-90s, we brushed sweat from our eyes, focusing our binoculars on an amazingly colorful array of birds in the fifteen locations we visited, from postage-stamp sized parks in city centers to remote national wildlife refuges. For those driven by numbers, these two neophyte bird watchers identified 123 species, 86 of which we had never seen before. We had a lot of help.

Birders are a very special breed. We would sidle up next to a couple with obvious birding experience (judging by clothes and equipment), and ask a simple question. What do you see?

A quick answer, tossed our way in an excited whisper, often led to an invitation to see the bird through their much-better binoculars and the opening of a bird book for a lengthy discussion of the bird's attributes, its plumage, where it wintered, the amazing journey it was now on, and how to distinguish it from similar birds.

Many of these birds are migrating north now and the Texas Coast is their first rest stop after a long flight over the Gulf of Mexico.

I thought about how different birders are from anglers. An angler wouldn't share a hot fishing tip or spot with his or her mother. Birders will tell you everything, eagerly. Birding, apparently, is a team sport. And it's a good thing, because we saw a whole lot of birds that never make it to Maine. Indeed, many of the nonmigrating birds we saw never make it north of the Rio Grande Valley.

There is a lesson here for Maine. Birding brings big bucks. Texas works to capture those bucks, with lots of advertising aimed at birders, a wonderful array of maps and brochures organized around day and week-long birding adventures, and many places to see these splendid creatures. Surprisingly, some of the best birding spots are sewage treatment plants. And they are listed in the birding guides!

The Rio Grande Valley is home to a million people and suffers one of the highest unemployment rates in the nation. One county has the lowest per capita income in the United States. They have wisely embraced the 150,000 to 200,000 birders who flock here, spending $240 million that supports 3000 jobs.

Here in Maine, some folks, especially Representative Bob Duchesne, are working to create a birding economy. Check out the MaineBirdingTrail.com website. We have unique birds and their economic potential is great. But we need infrastructure, targeted marketing, and good place-based information. The information available to us for our birding vacation in Texas, and the number of places eager for our visit, was impressive.

Maine can learn a lot from the big state of Texas, a place that successfully captures the allure and marketability of its smallest creatures. For you birders, here are a few tidbits to tantalize: Our Texas favorites: Painted Bunting, Indigo Bunting, Cerulean Warbler, Blue Grosbeak, Green Jay, Great Kiskadee, Altamira Oriole, Summer Tanager, Hepatic Tanager, Buff-bellied Hummingbird, Black-necked Stilt, Green Heron, Reddish Egret, and the world's tiniest sandpiper, the Least Sandpiper. It didn't look "least" to us, just tiny.

We saw Botteri and Olive Sparrows, Clay-colored Robins, unbelievable numbers of shore birds, four types of orioles, three types of rails, and 17 different warblers. We even saw wild Green Parrots.

Bird watching is a lot like treasure hunting. That's treasure with a capital T and that spells Texas. Forget the yellow rose of Texas. Go there to see the Yellow-headed Blackbird.

Update: Since I wrote this column in 2009, Bob Duchesne has published his wonderful Maine Birding Trail guide, and the Maine Tourism Commission has printed and distributed hundreds of thousands of them in brochure format. And more and more birders are coming here every year.

Birding in Big Bend National Park

Big Bend National Park is relentlessly stunning, high mountain desert alongside the Rio Grande, and a paradise for all who love the outdoors.

Linda

Big Bend is one of the most spectacular sights you will ever see. We've visited many national parks and this has become a favorite.

Picture hilly arid land with a backdrop of long mountain chains that take your breath away. Some formations create rounded sculpture shapes, while others are more angular. Rock variations color the hillsides in shades of taupe, red, and white. This is a geologist's dream and many travel here for that reason. I tell George that this is the polar opposite of Mount Vernon. It feels like you can see forever, and it's hard to take all this vastness in.

After our interminable winter, I am soaking in the heat here. Boy, it gets hot, even in April, where the average daytime temperature this week was 90. Hot, sunny, and dry, but it cools down into the fifties at night with a lovely breeze.

The desert scrublands are covered with plants completely foreign to us. There's a mixture of mesquite, acacia, and a variety of cactus. I love the giant yucca plants with their impressive white plumes rising out of their centers. Probably the strangest plant here is the ocotillo - stalks that look dead sport red blossoms on top, and if it rains the stalks are covered with little green leaves a couple days later.

Birding

Of all of the great national parks why do we come to Big Bend? It's a birder's paradise. More than 450 different species have been recorded here. Arriving in April we are able to see some migrating species as well as year-round and summer residents. The Rio Grande is a lush corridor through this desert land and a bird migration highway. The park is composed of grasslands, riparian oasis, river, mountains, and desert shrub habitats. Hitting all those areas turns up a wide variety of birds.

There's nothing quite like seeing the boldly patterned face of an acorn woodpecker looking at you, and then, a few feet away, lands a ladder-backed woodpecker. Their calls are loud and clear as they dart back and forth.

Imagine walking down to the Rio Grande and lifting your binoculars to capture a pair of summer tanagers in the same view - the male vibrant red and the female bright yellow. No, I'm not in Mount Vernon anymore! As I lather up with good sunscreen, pack a picnic and lots of water, I am able to anticipate incredible birds for hours on end - my idea of a perfect vacation.

George

On our first visit, we came here strictly to bird. We did not anticipate the beauty of the mountains and desert. The park is huge and we cover much of it. Spread throughout are tiny pockets of water that draw the birds.

It is not easy to get here from Maine. We drove to Portland, bussed to Boston, flew to Houston, flew to El Paso, stayed overnight there, then drove to Terlingua the next day. The last part of the drive follows the Rio Grande for 50 miles, and we get out often, spotting birds.

One day our friend Jim Kinney, a neighbor in Mount Vernon and a winter resident of Texas, joined us for a day in the Big Bend State Park nearby, and brought with him Cathy Hoyt, a butterfly, desert plant, bird, and archeology expert. She led us to an amazing oasis in the middle of the desert. What a tour guide!

Linda is right – the scale of things out here is hard to imagine for us Mainers. My favorite place is in the Chisos Mountains, where it's cooler, the hikes are manageable, the birds are plentiful, the scenery is jaw-dropping incredible, and they even have a nice restaurant. Paradise!

Lodging – George

Four years ago we could find only small motels in Terlingua, the town on the edge of the national park, so we stayed at a nice resort in neighboring Lajitas. But it was a longer drive to Big Bend, so this time, we looked for a place closer to the park.

And we really lucked out. I found Villa Terlingua on line, and Cynta de Narvaez, the owner, quickly replied to my emailed inquiry. She has one large 5-bedroom house and two smaller adjacent houses. Cynta is always on the premises and is a fascinating person, a former river guide, a community leader, and lots more. She was tremendously helpful before we went and especially while we were there.

For a guy whose new book is titled *A Life Lived Outdoors*, Villa Terlingua was somewhat ironic. Many people in Terlingua really do live life outside. Inside our neat little one-room house was a bed, kitchen, full-sized fridge, desk, table, and more, with a full bath in a cute little building next to the house. But almost all of these things were also outside, including a bed, sink, fireplace, grill, shower, tables and chairs, and a lovely couch and rocker.

Cynta spent 16 years building these homes out of a 90-year-old limestone ruin, and furnished them with antiques, books and collectables she picked up while traveling around the world.

I'm sitting on the porch, staring at the mountains of Big Bend to the east, writing this column, and a Bewick's Wren just walked into our courtyard, pranced around, and ate something. A few minutes ago, two dozen Lesser Goldfinches landed in a flowering bush to my right. A quail is calling not far away. This is birding heaven! And a rabbit just bounded by!

Lodging – Linda

I immediately fell in love with the house we rented this trip. It is in the Ghost Town section of Terlingua, but trust me, it's not spooky. The little house is decorated with a variety of eclectic things, and the outside living spaces are enclosed by rock walls of ancient stones. The open air feeling of sitting outside while a pleasant breeze blows through is a sure cure for stress. And then there's the view…lots of open land with enormous rock formations as a backdrop.

It took me a few days to figure out the time of day. The sun doesn't rise until after 7:00 a.m. We were sure to see the sunrise as well as the crescent moon and Venus, still visible in the morning!

Food – George

Lin loves to cook, so we ate all of our breakfasts and some of our dinners at the house. But the Starlight Theater, THE place to eat in Terlingua, is a five-minute walk across the cactus-crowded hillside, and we fell in love with the place when we visited four years ago.

The Starlight was originally constructed in the 1930s as the Chisos Movie Theater. Mining drove the local economy then. Now, they depend on tourists. In the 1960s, without a roof, the place once again offered theater performances for the locals, hence the name, the Starlight Theater. In 1999 the place got a facelift and roof and became a restaurant.

If you can remember what you had to eat in a place four years ago, it's gotta be pretty darned good! And we did. We'd been looking forward to the Starlight's unique and award-winning chili, so we each had that on our first visit, along with a large salad and locally brewed beers. The place was jammed, with a one-hour wait for a table, but we were lucky enough to spot and grab two places at the bar. The Starlight also has live music every night, so it's a very entertaining place.

On our second visit, I had something else I remembered, the chicken-fried antelope. It is soooo good. With a ton of mashed potato and some excellent veggies, this was a memorable meal.

The Starlight is next to a couple of stores where local folks gather on the porch every evening to enjoy the sunset. Someone is always strumming a guitar while the adults enjoy cold beverages and the kids play with hula hoops. Everyone faces east, rather than west where the sun is actually setting, so they can watch the sunlight – often pink – go up and over the mountains. It is a spectacular sight.

Linda – food

I too remembered that chili as extraordinary, and it still is. We actually ordered it twice this trip. Texas chili is very meaty and made without beans. I wish I knew the secret combination of seasonings. One night I got chicken, spinach and mushrooms in a cream sauce. That was a superb dish as well.

We shopped in Marfa for food supplies for the week. Having a kitchen and fridge let us enjoy our home away from home, and the Telingua Market had other supplies to keep us well stocked. Cooking there gave me one more pleasure – watching George wash dishes outside. He claimed he loved it, so maybe we'll try it at home!

Hoopoe hurray!

Don't die until you see a Hoopoe. What a stunning bird!

In Italy for the last two weeks of June, we saw many European Hoopoes, entranced by every single one.

Each morning we'd pull out our map and choose a walk on one of the ancient gravel roads that wind up, down, and over the hillsides that surrounded us in Greve, a Tuscany village about 45 minutes south of Florence.

Those walks took us past old homes, vineyards and olive groves, and through forests full of birds. I'm certain the locals made fun of the tourists with binoculars always stuck to their faces! We do a lot of birding in Italy.

On our first trip here a few years ago, we spotted a very colorful bird near a small stream that flows through the village. The bird was yellow, brown, and black with a bright red face. We thought we'd discovered a most amazing creature, so we raced back to our apartment to haul out our *Birds of Europe* book, only to discover that it was a very common European Goldfinch! I guess it must be a cousin to the dozens of Goldfinches that crowd our bird feeder at home all winter long.

My first look at a Hoopoe came on this most recent trip when Linda shook me awake at 7:00 a.m. on our first morning, almost shouting, "You've got to see this bird!" And I had to admit, it was magnificent. So I couldn't be grouchy about getting woken - even though I later learned that the Hoopoe is considered the "bird of ill omen." We suffered no bad luck.

And the next morning, there were five Hoopoes on the lawn!

Fictional tales (sort of)

The dead deer that wasn't

We'd been lifelong friends, and before I became a full-time Maine guide, I worked for him for a while in his Augusta lawn and garden retail store. But I never offered to take him on a professionally guided hunt, because it would have ruined my reputation. I did hunt with him a lot. And to protect his reputation, I'm not going to tell you his name. Let's just call him Bigfoot.

Bigfoot hunted through the woods like a raging bull moose. That's why we usually let him do the walking while we took stands up ahead of him, counting on him to drive the deer our way. He is a lot of fun to have on a hunt because he is very lucky and always manages to see deer, usually coming up with a novel way of failing to shoot one.

Back in the day, our favored hunting method was the deer drive. This involves sending a few hunters through the woods in a line, hoping to drive deer toward a few standers up ahead. Driving is legal in most states, but Maine, in its fastidiousness, has made it illegal. Many hunters still drive deer but I avoid it these days, not willing to risk my guide's license.

Anyway, when driving deer, we would place Bigfoot between two other drivers, hoping to slow him down and keep track of him. Didn't always work. I remember one drive when, half way to our finish line, we encountered Bigfoot coming back toward us. He'd already gotten to the finish and returned!

Occasionally, hoping fervently that he might finally shoot a deer, we would place him in a stand. One time, another guy in our hunting party escorted Bigfoot to his stand before moving on to another spot. We started the drive about a half mile away and about 200 yards from Bigfoot's stand, I jumped three deer. They headed right for Bigfoot and I eagerly listened for his shots. Dead silence.

When I got to the stand, Bigfoot was gone. Did he race off after the deer, I wondered? We looked for him briefly, then gave up, returning home for breakfast. Upon arrival at the house, there, at the kitchen table, chowing down on Linda's homemade blueberry muffins, was Bigfoot. He'd gotten hungry and abandoned his stand to get an early breakfast!

I've got a lot of Bigfoot stories, but here's one of my favorites. We'd still hunted a neighbor's woodlot all morning, Bigfoot starting on one end, me on the other, with nary a sighting, so I decided to try something different in the afternoon.

Knowing that he, on days like this with no wind and a soft understory for quiet walking, would still be heard about 200 yards ahead as he stalked through the woods, I decided to put him to work for me. We'd cover small pieces and try to get a deer moving toward one or the other of us. Truthfully, I assumed all the movement would be in my direction.

I sent Bigfoot off down a tote road, told him to go about 500 yards and then enter the bog on his left, go in there about 100 yards, turn left and hunt back to me. If that didn't work, we'd move up the woodlot about a quarter mile, and I'd do the walking while Bigfoot took a stand. Seemed very democratic to me.

I settled in, sitting on a stone wall where I could see about 75 yards into the bog, eagerly awaiting the big buck I hoped Bigfoot would send my way. I hadn't been seated very long when, out in the bog, I heard a shout.

Now, I had carefully instructed Bigfoot to avoid even whispering when we were hunting together, so a shout was shocking. But it was him, no question about it, although I couldn't make out what he'd shouted. A quick second later there was a shot, close enough that I jumped – and took cover.

Then more shouting. Only it was getting further and further away. Terrible thoughts ran through my mind. He'd shot himself and panicked. He'd shot someone else, and was running for help. While I stood there, not sure what to do, there was another shot – now so far away that I couldn't tell if he was still shouting.

I tore off toward the last shot, hustling along through the bog as fast as I could. As I approached the place where that last shot came from, I hoped to see Bigfoot. No luck. Not even a trace. And there were no more shots – no more shouts. The woods were silent. And I was scared.

So I started shouting. Using an imaginative vocabulary, I shouted his name, let him know how badly he'd messed up. And got no answer. Now I was really worried. If he had shot himself, how would I find him? Would he still be alive?

It was about 3:00 p.m., with just a couple of hours of light left, so I had to find him fast. Assuming he'd continued on in the same direction, I headed onward, up and out of the bog, toward a high ridge. I walked and hollered. Walked and hollered. No answer.

After 20 minutes, I crested the ridge, gazed down toward a stream that meandered through the valley about 300 yards from where I stood, and spotted the familiar orange cap, tipped back on the head of Bigfoot, who seemed to be very much alive, still moving away from me.

Not about to lose him now, I fired a shot. And he turned my way. No way was I going down there to get him, so I waved at him, signaling for him to come to me. And he did, arriving with his head down and sweat pouring off him.

He fell to the ground, sat with his back to a tree, took off his hat and unzipped his coat, and slowly told me his sad tale. It was hard to believe. I asked for proof. So we began the long hike back to where it all started, the place of the first shout, the first shot.

Pointing to the ground, Bigfoot exclaimed, "It was right there. I was walking quietly through the bog and when I got over by that small pine over there, I looked this way and saw it, lying right there." He'd been standing about 40 yards from the spot he pointed to.

Looking carefully at the spot, I saw a good deal of blood. Yes, a deer had lain here, bleeding badly.

Bigfoot had been plowing along when he saw a dark brown object lying here, in a heap under a small bush. Carefully and quietly approaching, at least to the best of his limited ability, he got within 10 yards and identified the object as a deer – a dead deer.

He walked a bit closer, lowered his gun, and shouted to me. "Hey Bill, there's a dead deer here!"

The "dead" deer, alerted to Bigfoot's presence, struggled up and limped off. Bigfoot was stunned. Punching off the safety on his rifle, he fired wildly from the hip at the doe, moving more quickly now through the bog. It was a clear miss and later I pointed out the tree that he'd hit. "Got yourself a tree, my friend," I told him.

Bigfoot charged off after the deer, tripped and fell, a couple of times, but amazingly, caught up with the poor thing, and got off another blast as well as another shout. Missed again.

This time the doe was getting desperate to escape and leaped into a fir thicket, tail down, a pretty good indication that she was really hurting. Bigfoot saw her dive into the thicket, ran to the side of it, and took another shot as she emerged. Another miss. In my confusion, I remembered hearing only two shots, but Bigfoot insisted he'd shot three times.

When the doe crested the ridge, she was gone. He would not see her again, even though he trudged after her, after taking a few minutes to collect himself.

I made him return with me to the ridge and show me the last place he'd seen her. Down on my hands and knees, I looked for blood, hair, anything that would lead us to where I was certain she now lay dead. There was no sign of her. And the ground was so hard and rocky, I couldn't even find a good track to follow.

For the final 30 minutes that day, Bigfoot and I traveled in concentric circles, on the other side of the stream, hoping to see her lying on the ground. No luck. With heavy hearts, we gave up as darkness settled in, unloaded our rifles, and began the long walk back to my vehicle.

I would have returned to continue the search the next morning, but a heavy rain that night washed away any chance we had of finding her. These days, there are several guides who will show up with dogs specially trained to find dead deer. If we'd had one that day, I am certain we'd have found that deer.

Thankful that Bigfoot was okay, but angry at the hunter who had wounded that deer and not looked for it, I am still, today, troubled by it all.

It was many years before Bigfoot actually shot a deer, and I always thought it was because he failed to take that deer when it was offered up, right there at his feet. But for a shout, it would have been his.

This is a work of fiction, based on real situations I have experienced while hunting with Bigfoot.

Ice fishing fiasco

Brian took the local Boy Scouts ice fishing once every winter. He fancied himself a good scout, although he'd never been a Boy Scout, and some of these boys never got outdoors, never mind gone fishing. That was the tragedy for kids these days – too much indoor time, not enough outdoor time.

"Say, Denny," Brian said one morning over coffee and muffins at the local cafe, "How's about we take them young'uns way up north this year? We might even do an overnight at that fancy sporting camp where Brad Fielder sometimes guides. Bet they'd give us a special deal for the scouts, and I'd like to see the place myself."

"I'm in!" exclaimed Snappy. "There's some great ice fishing waters up that way. I'll bring the bait!"

Denny sold bait, like a lot of rural Mainers, from out of his garage. Most of his customers didn't know an emerald shiner from a flat head minnow, so it was an easy business for Denny. Didn't matter what he caught. He could sell 'em.

'Course, some of those bait fish ended up alive in the state's wild trout waters, after fishermen dumped the remains of their bait buckets into the ponds before heading home, and those bait fish sometimes wiped out the wild trout in those ponds – but a guy's gotta make a living, right?

Brian called on Fielder for help and a date was soon set for this ice fishing adventure. Brian was flabbergasted when the owners of Camp Sourdnahunk, Frank and Phyllis Smith, offered to host the group for free. "Dang nab it!" he exclaimed. "I should a thought a this a long time ago!"

Brian whipped up a list of clothes and other instructions for each scout and delivered it to the parents, with contact info for those who had to be in constant contact with their kiddies, some of whom had cell phones. Brian didn't tell the parents that there was no cell phone coverage at the camp. No sense to get them all het up.

Two parents – both experienced ice anglers – volunteered to go with them, a big help considering there'd be a dozen boys to corral and keep track of. Some were real hellions. The parents, Bill Friedman and Pete Smith, were big guys and took no guff. Just what Brian needed on this trip. Denny was a pushover. The kids paid no mind to anything he told them. And they knew he was good for a laugh, or a treat. He carried lots of candy and constantly handed it out to the kids just like you'd feed biscuits to a dog. Actually, a dog would be more appreciative of a treat than some of these spoiled kids.

Brian, Denny, Bill, and Pete met parents and kids at the elementary school late on a Friday afternoon, loaded up the four vehicles that would transport them all to the camp, and started the long three-hour drive to Camp Sourdnahunk. They arrived in time for supper. That Phyllis was some old good at the wood cook stove, and everyone enjoyed the hearty venison stew – except for the two kids who claimed to be vegetarians. After a bit of a pep talk from Brian, those two kids dug into the venison stew like it was the best thing they'd ever eaten. In fact, they ate two big bowls of it and promised Brian they'd never tell their parents.

"I love turning kids on to wild meat," Brian told the other guys, "especially when their parents are pushing them away from it." Brian noticed that Bill and Pete were digging down deep too, lapping clean their third bowl of stew before moving on to Phyllis's chocolate cake. Phyllis's cake was not that fancy flourless kind either! And it had plenty of vanilla frosting to complement the vanilla ice cream.

The guys shepherded the kids to their respective cabins, made sure they were all in bed – funny thing about that, not a single kid said he had to brush his teeth before bed – then returned to the lodge to relax in front of the fireplace with a cold beer and tell each other lies and other stories.

Brian was a particularly good story teller and he kept the guys entertained for a couple of hours and several beers apiece. It was near 10:00 p.m. when they wore down, ready to get some sleep, knowing they'd have their hands full the next day.

Breakfast was scheduled for 8:00 a.m. but most of the kids were up well before that, eager to fish. They looked like quite a bunch, all bundled up in their cold weather gear. Brian was thankful that it was a nice day, sunny, temps in the high 30s, best it gets in that neck of the woods.

Brian and Denny had spent some time at home pouring over maps of the local ponds, and chosen one that both had fished once in the open water season. Brian double checked to make sure the chosen water, Frost Pond, was open to ice fishing.

It was easy enough to check. All waters closed to ice fishing were listed by county. So all Brian and Denny had to do was check out the list of waters in Piscataquis County, home to Frost Pond, in the ice fishing section of the fishing rule book. "Not there," stammered Denny. "We'll be good to go."

Now, Brian probably should have stepped back at that point and doubled checked. Maine's fishing rule book would confound a Philadelphia lawyer – in fact, many Mainers had taken great delight when a real Philadelphia lawyer was written up by a game warden last summer for violating an obscure fishing rule on the Kennebec River, where the rules changed about every few miles down the river. The rules just for the Kennebec – in very tiny print – took up four pages in the rule book. The lawyer thought he was in one section of the river but was in the next one down. He had kept a 14-inch brown trout, which would have been okay in the section he thought he was in, but not in the section where he actually caught the trout.

The fact that the lawyer was not well liked locally – he often rented a camp there and was a real prick – just made the offense all the better. He paid his fine and vowed never to return to Maine. "Good riddance," said Denny when Brian read him the news story. Brian wondered how many potential customers for Maine guides were turned off and away by the state's confusing hunting and fishing rules and – sometimes – heavy handed game wardens. Some wardens just didn't understand the importance of treating the state's visiting sports in a friendly manner.

Frost Pond was a short drive from the camps, and happily right alongside the tote road so snowshoes weren't needed to get on the pond. While the boys careened around the lake, firing snowballs at each other and building weird-looking snowmen, Brian, Denny, Bill, and Pete drilled two dozen holes before starting to set up the traps with bait. They were using Emeril shiners. At least Brian was sure of that.

Things were looking good when the first flag went up after the guys had only gotten six traps in the water. Denny yelled to the boys and rounded them up, letting one of them grab the trap, set the hook, and reel in the fish, a beautiful 10-inch brook trout.

Denny announced that it was a keeper – the minimum length limit on Frost Pond was 8 inches – and quickly tossed it into the cooler. They planned to keep enough so each boy could have one fish for supper.

And they were well on their way to that goal by 11:00 a.m. – with 10 brookies in the cooler including a big 14-inch beauty – when a game warden showed up.

Brian was delighted to see a game warden, and quickly gathered the boys around the warden for introductions. "These here are the Boy Scouts," Brian announced proudly. "Every one is an expert fisherman!"

Brian then introduced himself, Denny, Bill, and Pete, and only then became troubled that the warden had yet to tell them his name. "Kind of a rude guy," Brian thought to himself, but you never want to aggravate a man with a gun, so he kept his opinion to himself.

Finally, the warden said, "My name is Frederick Neal. And you guys are in a lot of trouble." Brian's heart sank when he heard those words. He saw his Maine guide's license going away, but more than that, he was embarrassed to be called out in front of the Scouts.

"What are you talking about," stammered Denny before Brian could come up with a proper response. "We've done everything legal, just like the rule book says!"

Brian quickly chimed in. "That's right. We made sure this water is open to ice fishing, carefully checked the length and bag limits, and we've only kept 10 fish. What did we do wrong?" His last sentence sounded more like a plea than a question.

"You're fishing on a pond that's closed to ice fishing," Neal announced with a grin on his face. He was really enjoying this.

"Wait a minute," said Brian, who was getting mad now, most particularly because of that grin on Neal's face. "And why are you smiling?"

"Show me your rule book," demanded Neal.

Brian went to his backpack and drew out the thick fishing rule book. He had circled Frost Pond in the section on Piscataquis County, and quickly drew the warden's attention to that.

"See, right over here is the list of waters that are closed to ice fishing," stammered Brian. "Frost Pond is not on that list." He was so sure he was right, he was starting to lose it.

"Well, that's where you're wrong," crowed Neal. "That's the list of waters that are open to ice fishing. All the rest of the waters in this county are closed - including Frost Pond. I've got you for fishing a closed water and for ten fish over your limit, and shame on you turning these young scouts into law breakers."

That's when Brian lost it. Charging toward the warden, he would have been in violation of a bunch of other laws if Bill and Pete hadn't jumped in to stop him before he got to Neal. Brian was salivating by then.

Bill, a lawyer, turned and tried a different approach with the warden. In his best lawyerly voice, Bill announced, "I am an attorney and I think there's some confusion over these lists."

"You're damned right there's some confusion," shouted Brian. "And this damned game warden's the one who's confused!"

Brian waved the rule book in the air before turning to his home county's page and pointing to the list of waters closed to ice fishing. "See this. This is the list of waters CLOSED to ice fishing in my county!" shouted Brian. Now keeping his distance, with his right hand on his pistol, Neal said, "That's right, in your county we list the waters closed to ice fishing. But in Piscataquis County, we list the waters that are open to ice fishing. Give me your license so I can write these summonses!" Neal seemed to be getting worked up too.

Brian handed his license to Bill who handed it to Neal who wrote two summonses, both in Brian's name. "I'm doing you a favor and only writing up you, Mr. Webster. I could give a summons to each of the adults and most of the kids. But I think you are really the one to blame for this."

"I'll tell you who's to blame!" shouted Brian. "It's you damned game wardens and your damned biologists and your damned department and your damned legislators! Even a Philadelphia lawyer can't understand all these stupid rules!"

Neal, who sensed that things might be getting out of control, turned to the scouts and told them it was time to pack up their traps and move on back to camp. Then he handed the summonses to Bill, grabbed the container of trout, and turned in the other direction, being careful to walk directly away from Brian.

By now, Brian knew he'd gone too far, and he felt especially bad for the boys. But they gathered up the traps, trudged out to the vehicles, and drove back to camp. The boys were strangely quiet. There would be no trout for supper that night.

Phyllis, however, came through with a delicious supper of braised moose steaks, beans, coleslaw, and corn bread, and after supper Bill gave the boys a thoughtful presentation of what had gone wrong, making sure that they understood that it was an honest mistake on Brian's part. Actually, by then, the boys had moved on and were well into their nighttime rituals featuring a lot of misbehavior.

"Too bad we can't give summonses for that," mumbled Denny. That gave Brian a grin. The toughest part was explaining it all to the parents, standing there in the elementary school parking lot on Sunday afternoon. Most seemed very sympathetic.

And the best news of all came about a week later, when Fish and Wildlife Commissioner Maynard Connors stopped by Brian's place to inform him that the summonses had been ripped up and a reprimand placed in warden Neal's file.

"Warden Neal handled that situation all wrong," Connors told Brian. "You made an honest mistake, Brian. And we are all going to learn from it because next year, I'm going to make sure that the waters closed to ice fishing are listed consistently for all counties. We'll call it Brian's list."

And that made Brian smile too.

Decoying the game wardens

Jack DeAngelis nearly lost his job as a deputy sheriff when he got nailed by game wardens for shooting at a huge buck standing near the road on posted land. Although Jack did almost everything right – including getting out of his truck, moving off the road before loading his rifle, and taking a careful shot at the buck – he made two critical mistakes.

DeAngelis shot at a deer on posted land. And the buck was a decoy, manufactured in the garage of game warden Chris Collier. Oh, it was a good-looking buck with a huge 8-point rack, a head that moved up and down, and a tail that twitched. Collier bragged that it would excite even the most honest hunter and maybe get him to make an illegal move.

"This will catch a lot of guys," laughed Collier, one of the many wardens who insisted – and seemed to really believe – that 95% of

215

hunters and anglers would break the laws and rules when they got a chance and thought they could get away with it.

Collier and his partner, Joe Fisher, were hidden in the bushes nearby and nearly scared Jack to death, after he fired at the buck, when they jumped out and shouted, in unison, "Drop the gun. You're under arrest!"

Joe turned toward them, stunned, but knew enough about law enforcement to comply, letting his rifle drop gently to the ground. "What the hell are you guys doing here," he asked?

"We got you, DeAngelis," crowed Fisher. "You're trespassing."

"What do you mean I'm trespassing? I got out of my truck, walked over here ten feet off the road, loaded the rifle, and shot that buck. I did everything right by the book," claimed Jack, shouting now, angry and distressed.

"I guess you didn't hear about that court case last year," laughed Collier. "The judge ruled that you can trespass with a bullet. Your bullet trespassed, DeAngelis, and you're done hunting."

Stunned by this revelation, Jack picked up his rifle and trudged dejectedly back across the road, stowing it in the truck, and returning for the summons Collier was now writing up for him. "I suggest you plead guilty and pay your fine," Collier told DeAngelis, "because a lawyer and trial will be expensive, and there's no way you are getting out of this."

And that's what DeAngelis did, a week later, after squaring things with the sheriff, a hunter himself who had never heard of bullet trespass. The sheriff actually called Colonel Woodcock of the Maine Warden Service to ask about it. Sure enough, in Maine now, you cannot shoot onto posted land. But as usual, the Department of Inland Fisheries and Wildlife hadn't done much to publicize this fact, leaving hunters susceptible to arrest and prosecution.

Many of DeAngelis's hunting buddies and friends, including Snappy and Big Gus, were outraged by the lack of professional respect shown by the wardens to a fellow police officer — and by the whole idea of bullet trespass which none of them had heard of. After a few heated discussions over beers at their favorite pub, they hatched a scheme to turn the tables on Collier and Fisher.

The scheme took root when Snappy was telling the guys about a fella in Texas who had invented remote control hunting. The guy had put a trail camera out on his ranch, along with a rifle controlled remotely from his house. The camera broadcast directly to his computer, so the guy could watch the game trail and, when he saw the deer he wanted, fire the rifle remotely.

Although he'd originally created this for himself, he quickly realized he could set up guided hunts for anyone on the planet. All they had to do was have a computer and lots of money. You could now sit in Mount Vernon, Maine, and shoot a big buck on a Texas ranch, without getting off the couch.

The guy in Texas was raking in the dough, while some states scrambled to figure out how to make his scheme illegal in their states. Gus had heard that the Maine Sportsman's Association was going to propose a law to make this illegal in Maine. But it wasn't illegal yet.

It really didn't take long for the guys to build this idea into an imaginative way to turn the tables on the wardens who busted their friend DeAngelis. Gus, not wanting to risk his guide's license, begged off, leaving the planning to Snappy and the boys, but only after adding a couple of nice touches to the plan.

So one night the guys gathered in Jeff Caban's heated garage to build their own decoy. Skip Trask, who worked as a computer programmer for the state's largest website consultant, figured out how to set the whole thing up on his computer, and the game was on.

They had to hurry because there was only one week left in the deer hunting season. On the other hand, guys were getting desperate to get their deer, so it would be easy to convince wardens that night hunters were out and about.

In a local field on Bowens Hill – unposted, they made sure of that – they got to work just after dark on a Thursday night, setting up their decoy deer, lights, and rifle. Then they went to Skip's house to enjoy burgers and beer in his game room and get ready for the fun to begin.

They'd greased the skids by having anonymous calls placed to the Warden Service's hot line for the last three nights running, claiming shots were being fired at night in the Bowens Hill field. Although they couldn't guarantee it, the guys were pretty sure that Collier and Fisher had taken the bait and would be hiding that night not far from the field, parked in their truck about 50 feet up a snowmobile road that ran up alongside the field.

Just to be sure, they sent an unnamed ally – no, no, they would never have asked Jack DeAngelis to do this – who slowly poked his way into the nearby woods, in camo and black face paint, to verify that, yes, indeed, the wardens were staked out there.

When the ally called in the news, laughter and cheering erupted in Skip's game room. Game on! This was way better than any Patriot's game.

Promptly at 9:00 p.m., the game began. First, Skip activated the lights, flooding the field around the buck and lighting him up like a Christmas tree. Seconds later, he hit the button that remotely fired two shots – blanks, to keep this exercise as safe as possible.

Skip had also set up a remote-controlled camera that was linked to his TV screen, and the guys went wild when they saw Collier and Fisher running into the field. Although they couldn't hear the wardens, they could tell they were stunned as they ran up breathless to the deer and discovered it was a decoy.

You didn't even need to be able to read lips to know that Fisher shouted, "What the hell?" Blinded by the light, they dashed in that direction, shouting at the hunters they were sure were stationed there in the woods.

The wardens spent some time beating the bushes for the poachers, before returning to the place the lights hung from trees and discovering the rifle, set on a pedestal. At that point, Collier and Fisher began to understand that they'd been had. And they were mad. They pulled their own pistols and shot out the lights, grabbed the rifle, and kicked over the deer before returning to the truck.

Thinking they'd keep the rifle until someone claimed it and confessed to setting the wardens up, they were very surprised to be instructed, a few days later, to come to the Colonel's office and bring the rifle with them.

"Well, guys, it's like this," said Colonel Woodcock. "A landowner is accusing you of shooting out his lights, destroying a deer decoy he had in his field, and stealing his rifle. But it's your lucky day, because he's not going to press charges if you return the gun. So you are going to leave the gun here. I'll get it back to its owner.

"But I am putting a reprimand in your files and telling you one thing that you better never forget. Police officers – every one of them – deserve your courtesy and respect. I expect – actually insist – that you remember this in the future. Jack DeAngelis is a good man and a very good officer. Shame on you both. Now, get out of here and do your jobs."

When Collier and Fisher had left, Woodcock walked with the rifle down the hall to the conference room, where Jack DeAngelis was sitting, enjoying a cup of coffee and blueberry muffin with his pals Big Bob and Grouchy.

"I want to apologize to you again, Jack," said the Colonel, "and I hope you got a lot of enjoyment out of the payback administered by your friends. I trust you guys can return this rifle to its owner."

"Indeed I can, Charlie. And if you want, I can get you a copy of the whole escapade. The guys taped it. It's amazing what can be done by a smart guy with a computer," said Jack.

"I'll take it," responded the Colonel. "And use it in our training courses."

That brought a big smile to Jack's face.

About the Author

George A. Smith of Mount Vernon has done a lot of things in his life, from writing comprehensive plans for rural Maine towns to managing statewide referendum campaigns. He served as executive director of the Sportsman's Alliance of Maine for 18 years, growing the membership from 4,000 to 14,000 and making it one of the state's most influential organizations. George left SAM at the end of 2010 to write full time.

He writes an outdoor news blog posted on his website and the website of the *Bangor Daily News*, which was cited by the Maine Press Association in 2014 as the state's best sports blog. He has written a weekly editorial column published in the *Kennebec Journal* and *Morning Sentinel* of Waterville for 27 years, columns for *The Maine Sportsman* magazine since 1977, and special columns for the newsletters of various Maine organizations.

In 2014, Islandport Press in Yarmouth published *A Life Lived Outdoors*, a book of George's favorite columns about home, camp, family, faith, travel, hunting, fishing, and other outdoor activities. You can access much of George's writing on his website: georgesmithmaine.com.

George and his wife Linda, a recently retired first grade teacher, have written a weekly travel column for the *Kennebec Journal* and *Morning Sentinel* for five years, focused on Maine inns, restaurants, events and activities. Islandport Press published George and Linda's Maine travel book featuring their favorite inns and restaurants in 2016.

George also wrote a book about Maine sporting camps, which was published by Down East Books in 2016.

For 13 years, George and his friend Harry Vanderweide hosted a unique television talk show called *Wildfire* focused on hunting, fishing, conservation and environmental issues.

George was part of the management team that successfully defended Maine's moose hunt in a 1983 referendum, and he managed a successful campaign in 1992 that placed the Department of Inland Fisheries and Wildlife in the Maine Constitution and protected its revenues. He also led a successful campaign in 2004 to defeat a referendum that sought to end Maine's bear hunt. Among his many ideas, Smith conceived the Maine Outdoor Heritage Fund, financed by a Maine State Lottery instant ticket game, that has provided more than $18 million for wildlife conservation and outdoor recreation programs in Maine.

George is a Winthrop, Maine, native, a graduate of the University of Maine, and has lived in Mount Vernon for 39 years. He and Linda have three children and four grandchildren. George served five years on the Winthrop Town Council, three terms as Mount Vernon selectman, one term as Kennebec County commissioner, seven years on the Mount Vernon Planning Board, and 38 years as a trustee of the Dr. Shaw Memorial Library.

At the state level, George served on the Forest Legacy Advisory Committee, Maine Outdoor Heritage Fund Board, Commission to Study Trespass Laws, Hatchery Commission, Submerged Lands Task Force, Great Ponds Task Force, and many other task forces and study groups.

George Smith
34 Blake Hill Road
Mount Vernon, ME 04352
207-293-2661

georgesmithmaine@gmail.com   www.georgesmithmaine.com

www.ingramcontent.com/pod-product-compliance
Lightning Source LLC
Chambersburg PA
CBHW031130090426
42738CB00008B/1030